Purpose to Author-ity

PROFIT FROM WRITING ABOUT YOUR LIFE-PASSION

CaZ

Copyright © 2016 by Candy Zulkosky, aka CaZ

All rights reserved.

No part of this publication may be reproduced, distributed or transmitted in any form or by any means, including photocopying, recording, or other electronic or mechanical methods, without the prior written permission of the publisher, except in the case of brief quotations embodied in critical reviews and certain other noncommercial uses permitted by copyright law. Requests to the Publisher for permission should be addressed to the Permissions Department online at http://www.bytespress.com/booksupport/permissions.

For general information about our other products and services, please contact our Customer Care Department online at http://www.bytespress.com/booksupport

Bytes Press Publishing publishes in a variety of print and electronic formats and by print-on-demand. Some material included with standard versions of this book may not be included in e-book or in print-on-demand. If this book refers to media such as a CD or DVD that is not included in the version you purchased, you may download this material at http://www.bytespress.com/booksupport

Limit of Liability/Disclaimer of Warranty: While the publisher and author have used their best efforts in preparing this book, they make no representations or warranties with respect to the accuracy or completeness of the contents of this book and specifically disclaim any implied warranties of merchantability or fitness for a particular purpose. No warranty may be created or extended by sales representatives or written sales materials. The advice and strategies outlined herein may not be suitable for your situation. You should consult with a professional where appropriate. Neither the publisher nor the author shall be held liable for damages arising herefrom.

Purpose to Author-ity/ CaZ —1st ed.
ISBN-10: 0-9974709-3-3
ISBN-13: 978-0-9974709-3-2

Contents

Dedication iii

Foreword iv

Acknowledgements viii

Why This Book 1

What is Life-Passion? 8

What Is Author-ity? 13

Choose a Happiness Attitude 22

Seek and You Shall Find 36

The Dynamic You 42

Your Personality Strengths 51

Fear—It IS Personal... Don't Mistake It for Anything Else 67

Passion and Purpose 76

Recognize Life-Passion 81

Lights, Camera, Action 87

Prepare for Change 91

Write a Book in Two Weeks 97

How to Write a Book in 40 Hours 100

How to Hire a Writer 105

Words That Compel 114

When Should You Hire a Freelance Writer 123

Get Started on Publishing and Marketing 126

A Step-by-Step Guide to Publishing... 131

An Overview of Selling and Marketing Your Book 140

A Few Thoughts in Closing... 145

Dedication

For my sweet Robert. You light up my life in much the same way you light up a room when you enter. I had given up hope of having a life-partner until you danced your way into my life. Thanks for all you do.

And for Andy and Randy. This is so not your kind of book, but I know that both of you would have taken a copy to the Olde Barge, slapped it down on the bar, and proudly announced, "My sister wrote that!".
I miss you both. Every day.

Dedication

Foreword

What is it that fills you with wonder and color and brings vibrancy to your day? What inspires you to want and to do more? What is it that, if gone tomorrow, deep in your heart you could not bear losing?

Purpose to Author-ity explores your answers to these questions and more. CaZ shows the reader how to get in touch with passions and dreams that, together with purpose and action, become life-passions. Finding passion and living with purpose go hand-in-hand.

More than that, CaZ has written a book that takes the reader a step beyond self-exploration and understanding to the magic of telling (and sharing!) their story.

Everybody has a story—a story worth telling.

There is a book inside of you that wants to get out and be given to the world. Purpose to Author-ity is about bringing to light and fruition a hidden desire that many share: becoming an author. CaZ wrote this book following her own life-passion. She has learned the power of stories that are wrapped in purpose and passion; stories that share dreams and fulfillment.

In this book, CaZ offers concepts and guidance that will move the reader beyond searching, beyond reading, and beyond discovery to embrace their future. CaZ, in Purpose to Author-ity, has provided the tools needed to find your unique story and release that hidden book.

What specific life-challenges do you face? Are you searching and not even sure what you're searching for? Perhaps you're working in a job or career that once thrilled you and now bores and frustrates you? Are you tired of working for someone else and watching your bosses line their pockets on your efforts?

Maybe you are looking for an exciting business idea. Or it might be that you own a business and have found that was supposed to free you, has turned into a j-o-b. It might even be that you've created a financially successful business that leaves you with an emotional and spiritual hole where your joy should be. Do you have a hobby or activity that inspires you, that you absolutely love doing, that you find yourself thinking about even when you should be focused on other tasks? Do you wish that your life could be more exciting, have more freedom, or be more fulfilling?

Are you a writer frustrated by the conflict between your need to write and your need to earn a living that provides a quality life, or at least pays the bills consistently?

This last scenario describes the path CaZ stood upon when she chose to be a professional writer. Her journey toward living a purpose-filled life has not been a straight path, rather a long and often stumbling walk up hills and around curves with many crossroads allowing time to pause and ponder.

I met CaZ in 2006 at a time when I was at a crossroad. One of many pivot points in my life where I was faced with what felt like a sink or swim choice. I had just finished my certification as a coach from the Coaches Training Institute, and I saw a vast ocean of people just like me struggling to launch a business, and find a niche worthy of our natural strengths and gifts. Like me, many were bombing financially, and I was determined to find the convergence of passion, purpose and profit.

CaZ and I participated in an online course that helped students turn their expertise and knowledge into online courses. We connected by phone one day and that conversation quickly revealed that CaZ had all the skills and strengths I needed to help my business thrive. She is blessed with an uncanny ability to listen, to distill and simplify, to turn complex information into readable prose, and to find the right technology to support the heart and soul of any project.

The paths we chose from there have converged and diverged many times, and I credit CaZ for helping turn my business, She Negotiates, into the success it is today. Writing, whether it's news articles, blog posts, marketing copy, video courses, or training workbooks, is at the core everything I do as an executive coach and negotiation consultant, and I'm grateful for CaZ's contribution to a movement that is helping thousands of women find their place at the table.

It's no surprise that CaZ turned her gifts as a writer and teacher into the book you're reading now. There comes a time in any journey of exploration where decision and action are called for. That is the truth that this book embodies. Find the story within you and tell it.

Lisa Gates is a negotiation consultant and executive coach who knows how to bridge the gap between self-worth and net worth. As co-founder of She Negotiates, she delivers her company's signature courses, Strategic Conversations and Career Oxygen, both onsite and online. Lisa is the author of four video courses available online at lynda.com, including Asking for a Raise, Negotiation Fundamentals, Conflict Resolution Fundamentals and Coaching and Developing Employees.

She has been a frequent contributor to Forbes Woman, The Daily Muse and LinkedIn, and the work of She Negotiates has been featured on NPR, CNN, Fox, and in publications such as the New York Times, Wall Street Journal, More Magazine, and Real Simple, among others.

Acknowledgements

There are so many to thank and not enough room on the page.

Thanks to Lisa Gates, Susan Parsons Knab, Tonja Waring, and Gary Barnes. I am grateful for the part each of you played in the creation of this book and especially for your friendship and presence in my life.

Thanks to my family of friends, online and off. You know who you are.

And finally, thank you Mother and Daddy.

CHAPTER 1

Why This Book

"If you create and market a product or service through a business that is in alignment with your personality, capitalizes on your history, incorporates your experiences, harnesses your talents, optimizes your strengths, complements your weaknesses, honors your life purpose, and moves you towards the conquest of your own fears, there is absolutely no way that anyone in this or any other universe can offer the same value that you do."

—Walt Goodridge

"Know your purpose. Explore your life-passions. Use who you are, what you know, and what you love to create the life and lifestyle of your choosing."

—Candy Zulkosky

Did you know that 74 percent of employees believe happiness should be the most important reason for working? I think it is sad that these same people ALSO say that in the real world, in their world, happiness falls dead last in importance when it comes to choosing and staying with a job.

Think about that. Two-thirds of people want to be happy in their work (and, by inference in their lives) but are not.

I was stunned and distressed when I understood that so many people face this depressing daily reality. More than that, boy did it bring back memories.

I was one of those people. Quite suddenly, this statistic gave me a fresh appreciation for the depth of the trap I escaped when I struck out on my own as a freelance writer and entrepreneur. It was one of those epiphany moments that we all have upon occasion; right then I decided to find a way to help change this reality for anyone who wants it changed. This book is the result of that commitment to facilitate change.

Would you rather be among the 26 percent who choose happiness?

I would. I am. You can be, too. You've taken an important step by picking up this book.

What has brought you to this point? What is it that you hope and expect to take away? Do you face time pressures? Financial pressures? Do you struggle daily to maintain a balance between home and work? Are you a workaholic? Have you lost your spirit? Do you dream of a different, more fulfilling life? I'm willing to bet that you face one or more of these challenges.

Living life with purpose and passion, finding the right work, finding your calling, working for a purpose in a profession of your choosing, and starting your own business: all are worthy goals, but what is right for you? Not an easy question to answer. Life is complex today, more so than it was fifteen, ten, or even five years ago.

Now, more than ever, it takes preparation to thrive rather than survive.

This book is about you, your choices, and a method for sharing what drives you—your passion and purpose—with the world. Change and growth take place when you extend yourself to step forward and dare to let purpose, passion, and a moderate amount of risk into your life.

Together we will:
- Identify your knowledge, skills, and abilities,
- Explore your personal characteristics,
- Examine your experience and experiences,
- Identify your passions and home in on one significant and purposeful life-passion,
- Enable you to share your purpose and life-passion by becoming a published author.

Throughout the book there are activities described that will help you to know and appreciate yourself as well as your passions. When you devote time to understanding your gifts and talents, you develop a stronger sense of who you are, what you can contribute, and how you can continue to learn.

What Makes This Book different?

With this book, I've incorporated a belief and passion of mine—that we learn best when we teach. I'm often asked how I am able to work from home, how I knew how to turn my passion into a purposefully driven business. Helping you to identify and align your life-passion with purpose is a central premise in this book. It one of the main reasons I wrote it and, one hopes, an important reason for you to read this book.

Is this a new premise? In as much as it comes from my perspective, yes. Otherwise, no. There are other books that discuss passion and purpose. However, I have, in this book, taken the premise a step further to explain how, once you have identified your life-passion, to purposefully share that life-passion with others by being a published author.

As you gain clarity about passion and purpose, your life-purpose, this book will provide step-by-step guidance to enable you to share and profit by becoming a published author. I believe strongly that we experience purpose and passion more fully and find more meaning in our life-passions when we share the experience, and we benefit by seeing our life-passion through their lens. By gifting your knowledge, you tell your story and, coincidentally, learn even more about yourself and your passions.

I won't lie to you. This is not a book for a quick read at the beach. It takes effort to be serious about change and get clear about what you want. There are many steps in the publishing process—you may even decide that it's easier in the end to outsource the publishing part or go with a traditional publisher.

It takes courage to commit to experimenting with your life; and it takes time. If you are looking for a magic formula or a fix-it-quick BAND-AID®, then you've chosen the wrong venue. I don't believe such things exist, even though many search long and in vain for the easy road to success. It takes real commitment to transform your life in any meaningful way and just as much commitment to share that transformation with others.

This book asks you to think. The thinking part is voluntary. It may be that the full process asks more than you are willing to commit. Research has shown that as many as 90 percent of seekers looking for personal fulfillment see no improvement in their lives. Be in the other ten percent. Research has also shown that only half of the readers who pick up this book will finish it.

Take the time to learn, internalize, and implement the concepts presented here. Read and experience this book—and finish it. It is by your own efforts that you will achieve and exceed your personal, business, and financial goals.

My goal for you, my goal for this book is both hugely important and simple. I intend that you identify a means to become clear about what you want in order to maximize your potential and share your experience through your own words in print.

This is Why This Book

There are many books and courses devoted to helping you to identify your passion, to feel your dream, to become all you want to be. It seems likely, if you've picked up this book, that you've read some of the others, too. What I expect and hope you will do with this book is to move beyond the search, move beyond the reading, move beyond the discovery, and embrace the future you'd like to live.

Will you find all of your answers in this book? No book has all of the answers to all the questions. This book is part of a larger process. Identifying and understanding purpose and passion is a step in every personal growth program, but it is only one step. Entwining your passion with your life in a meaningful way so that your actions support purpose and elicit a positive impact on all that you are and do is vitally important to your success—personally and professionally. It is also a part of the process that is completely overlooked by many success gurus.

There comes a time in any journey of exploration where decision and action are required. That is the truth that this book embodies. Your focus will include discovery and growth. Your focus will also include possibilities for taking action and instruction for successful implementation.

I hope that this is the time in your journey for decision action. I came to that point (and probably will again!). This book has emerged from my experiences. I was a writer feeling frustrated by the conflict between my need to write and the inevitable need to earn a living. I was thirty-some years old and on my own for the first time in my life, struggling to come to terms with the loss of my husband and life partner.

I had recently left a reliable but dead-end corporate career for the risky world of employment in a medium-sized business. You know, one of those 'Girl-Friday' jobs where you wear every hat conceivable for less pay than you are worth because you truly like the job and the business owner? And where you worry about whether or not your next paycheck will bounce or even be written.

The light in my life at this time was my writing. Somehow, I managed to balance my career and creativity and continue to write. I wrote a weekly newspaper column, was working on a novel and short fiction, belonged to some fabulous writers' groups, and gained significant freelance technical writing experience and credits all while balancing my new career in marketing, printing, and publishing. Then the unimaginable happened. The job disappeared. My marketing consultant employer closed her business.

The light in my life through this second dark time remained my writing. I made a choice then, one that I've never regretted. I chose not to look for another job. I chose to focus on my writing, on my creative skills, on my natural ability to teach, and on my desire to help others. I became a full-time freelance writer and entrepreneur.

In his book *Self Matters*, Dr. Phil describes ten defining moments, seven critical choices, and five pivotal people in each life. Looking back, it is clear that the choice to go freelance was a turning point for me, one of those ten defining moments. Without understanding exactly what I was doing or why, I chose my purpose, I followed my life-passion and took the risky path toward fulfillment rather than the safe path toward comfort.

It has been and continues to be a journey. I've been fortunate enough to achieve wonderful successes. Along the way, my journey has included loss, failure, and numerous wrong turns yet also tremendous fulfillment and the discovery of my own power and inner strength. I've made mistakes and also done much that turned out to be very right.

This book echoes many of my experiences. Without consciously setting out to do so, I found my purpose and continue to live the life I chose, fully involved in activities that excite, inspire, and invigorate me.

If you find empathy in my situation or you fit any number of scenarios similar to those I've outlined previously, then step out onto a new path in your journey, one that homes in on the fulfillment you most desire. By sharing lessons from my journey, I can help you to find your successes and bypass my mistakes.

Let's identify your life-passion and your dreams for success and explore how you can move from Purpose to Author-ity. Let's write it down and tell the world about it.

Chapter 2

What is Life-Passion?

"Life-Passion comes from the heart; it melds core passion with the power of a destination. Purpose is power. Finding focus and taking action as a purpose powered person uses the energy and emotional fuel found in life-passion and is a true formula for success."

—Candy Zulkosky

A business idea based on anything but a life-passion is primed for failure. Purpose and life-passion are linked on many levels, none more compelling than when a life-passion leads to acting with purpose.

In my experience, passion is the most critical component in any occupation. Successful undertaking and completion of any project, whether for business or pleasure, requires passion applied to succeed. There is a huge void when the guidance provided by life-passion and purpose is lacking.

Life-passion is not something that you find once and have it forever. Life-passion is a choice and there are no rules that say you can't have more than one, even at the same time! Your life-passion and your purpose will evolve as you grow and evolve as a person and as life happens to, around, and with you.

I love the sea. One of the many amazing creatures that I've been fortunate enough to observe while spending time in, on, around, and under the ocean is the starfish. When I was five-years-old, my cousin gave me a starfish during a family trip to Florida. It was a real starfish, dried up of course, and I treasured it. When I was in my thirties and going through a difficult time, I saw a living starfish in its natural environment on the ocean floor and realized how incomplete my childhood treasure was. I did not value my own starfish any less, but suddenly I appreciated possibilities that I never knew existed in something I saw every day.

Life-passion is like that. It is always there; a part of you. Perhaps it is dried up. Yet it waits for you to provide the environment in which it will flourish.

Doors open when a life-passion is ignited and shared. The possibilities of your passion may not be immediately obvious to you. It takes conscious understanding and acknowledgement for the possibilities inherent in life-passions to bloom.

It was a simple, bottom-dwelling creature of the sea that helped me to understand the important combination of life and passion and purpose. Given life, the starfish crawls, walks, and glides along the ocean bottom. We're not starfish, but we too crawl, walk, and even glide through our daily lives. It takes passion and purpose for us to soar. That's what life-passion is; the juxtaposition of passion and purpose.

It takes life-passion for us to soar.

Life-Passion

Life is a vibrant and feeling experience. Passion provides power and emotion in life and is often experienced as a feeling of boundless enthusiasm, or (as is arguably the most common experience), an object of love.

Experiencing life-passion provides fuel to ignite enthusiasm and joy. Life-passion provides a *joie de vivre* unlike any other experience.

Life-passion fuels the imagination and gives courage. Life-passion steps beyond self-imposed boundaries.

Each of us is capable of choosing and experiencing many passions in a lifetime (and most of them are not romantic). Passions drive our successes and our failures. Passions are intimately involved in all of our life endeavors, and while we can pretend that passion and purpose are missing from our lives, the reality is that they never leave us. We do, however, misplace them.

A life-passion is an especially powerful combination that, once acted upon, ignites a powerfully consuming purpose.

I love what becomes possible when we recognize and know our life-passions and become involved every day in expressing our life-passions. It's all about the dream and living your dream. Passion has its own energy, an observable, transferable energy that can't be faked. It's an energy that shapes existence and opens the heart and mind to change.

A hidden or suppressed life-passion is sorrow. Not allowing yourself to follow your dreams and being afraid to embrace your life-passions are actions that eat away at you and cause bitterness, anger, and self-loathing. I know this from personal experience. Do you?

Following your dreams—that is freedom. Even when it's hard or scary and you feel like giving up—even then, there's something about following your heart's passion that feels right and purposeful. Your life-passions contain deep emotions, feelings that speak to your heart and make you feel purposefully alive.

When following a life-passion path, you can do what seems impossible and succeed. Yet, understand it's not about reckless abandon, rather, when you choose the path defined by life-passion, you follow your heart's desire without the interference of fear. Note the key words: *…without the interference of fear.* Fear only stops your dream if you let it.

Each of us will embrace and put aside many dreams and passions in life. I don't believe there should be only ONE life-passion experience; that road leads to obsession, which is not a healthy path to walk.

I have experienced many life-passions thus far. Some have become more important, more real to me than others. Some I put aside because the time wasn't right, or my focus changed, or I chose a different path. There is purpose in the way this works out, albeit the purpose is not always readily understood.

Life-Passions Include Purpose

Any phrase when repeated so often that it becomes accepted and expected becomes a cliché. Life is a Journey, while clearly a cliché, still retains its high value. Clichéd or not, it offers a truism that can't be denied. *Life IS a journey*. It is the choices we make along the way that negate the cliché to bring unique perspectives and individualism to each journey.

It seems to me that the choices we don't make (or at least aren't aware that we're making), the choices that seem forced upon us, often have the most impact on our lives. I have found that these are also the choices that lead us away from our passions and purpose. These are the choices that dampen our spirit and deny our dreams.

This book has a focus on positive emotion and enthusiasm. Make sure that experiencing your life-passion is an active part of your life. Life-passions are not meant to be hidden away, ignored, or put off until the right chain of events lines up.

I don't claim to know why we are here in this wonderful world, how the paths we follow through life are laid out for us, or what the ultimate purpose to my life, yours, or anyone's might be. I do know that I've lived my life both with passion and purpose entwined in my daily routine, and without. It's way better *with*. The journey is more pleasurable, easier, and simply makes more sense when purpose and passions are embraced as fulfilling life-passions.

By now, I hope you are asking yourself, *what is MY life-passion?* And perhaps other questions such as, *Why should I care what a life-passion is?* or *Who would care enough about my purpose to read my book?* and *Why is what I believe important enough to write about?* and *How do I go about finding and benefiting from my life-passion?*

Answers will become clearer as we journey together through these pages. The pathways of self-discovery and success lead to understanding and then sharing your life-passions with the world as a published author.

CHAPTER 3

What Is Author-ity?

"If you can't figure out your purpose, figure out your passion. For your passion will lead you right into your purpose."

—Bishop T.D. Jakes

Author-ity. I love the clarity of this word. It combines two important concepts and makes their correlation immediately identifiable. You are an authority, an expert, at something. You are an author when you, as an authority, have published your expertise.

I have no way of knowing what your particular expertise is, but I trust that you have knowledge and experience to share and a desire to empower others by sharing what you know.

I trust also that you are selling yourself short and struggling with identifying or sharing your life-passion.

And I trust that you likely don't have the foggiest idea of how to go about writing and publishing a book.

We'll do it together, beginning with learning about what your life-passions are, then how to get a book written, and finally, how to get that book published and marketed.

Writing and publishing a book is not as daunting as it seems to the uninitiated. If you can create a proper outline, you can write a book in 40-50 hours. In later chapters, I've included a proven, step-by-step process you can follow to take your knowledge of whatever your passion might be and turn it into a book.

Publishing is also a step-by-step process, and you need not wait for a publisher to pick you up. In later chapters, I also tell you how to publish your book, including self-publishing if that's your choice.

But I'm Not a Writer, How Can I Be an Author?

We live and work in an information age, a time where, for many professions and businesses, success or failure hinges on what you publish. Today your published message must do double duty: it must create the impression you want and elicit a response.

Repeat after me:

YOU DO NOT HAVE TO BE A WRITER TO BE AN AUTHOR.

YOU DO NOT HAVE TO LOVE WRITING TO WRITE A BOOK.

What you have to do is decide on your topic, choose what story you will tell in your book, and identify who you believe will benefit from reading your story.

What about passion? Do you have to be passionate about writing a book? Not about the writing part, but you want to be passionate about the subject of your book. That's why this book provides guidance to explore your life-passion with the goal of identifying how to communicate that passion to your chosen audience.

You already know everything you need to know to write your book. If you are comfortable writing, simply sit down and start.

If you prefer not to write it, then get it written for you by a professional writer. I've dedicated an entire chapter in this book to the process of hiring a professional writer, including knowing whether you should.

Decide to Publish

Have you decided to publish a book? Are you still on the fence? You know you have a book in you. Writing a book consistently appears on lists of top ten goals and dreams in life. Is it on yours? Have you decided?

If you are still on the fence, there's no reason for concern. Wanting to publish, having the dream of being published is enough for now. Deciding to publish involves first understanding the benefits that come from being a published author-ity, recognizing what your motivation is, defining your purpose, your reason for publishing a book, and—arguably the hardest—choosing the topic.

There are any number of reasons to publish. Perhaps the most obvious is the author-ity factor. When you are a published author, people see you in a different way, their first impression of you is different. You instantly become trustworthy, or more so than you were a moment ago when you were just anybody. It's a subconscious reaction, a validation of author-ity and your expertise.

There's also a recognition factor. Authoring a book helps you to get media and press attention, thus helping you expand your personal brand. Ever wonder how *expert* folks show up on TV talk shows or the morning news shows? Well, almost all of them will have published a book that enhanced their chance of being recognized as an expert in their field.

This author-ity recognition works well for any profession. If, for instance, you are a coach, speaker, trainer, or consultant, it's likely you already have written or have considered writing a book. Any number of other professions find authorship equally as compelling.

Consider how many politicians have either risen to fame or raised their recognition quotient by writing a book about themselves and some pivotal moment or passion in their life.

Winston Churchill won the Nobel Prize for Literature. Barack Obama, Bill Clinton, Jimmy Carter, Hillary Clinton, Sarah Palin, Newt Gingrich, Al Gore, Ted Kennedy, and John McCain are only a few of the contemporary politicians who are published. It's not a new trend. Ulysses S. Grant, Benjamin Disraeli, and Theodore Roosevelt each penned and published one or more books.

Publishing a book also helps in negotiation and winning client projects, both by lending credibility and in positioning yourself or your business. What is gained after you become an author is more than what you expect or imagine it to be.

Benefits of Publishing a Book

First, consider the *why*, specifically YOUR why. Your reason for writing a book comes from the heart, from your passion to serve a purpose. If not, then even a professional, seasoned writer will find writing your book to be a challenge. Aside from any fear or misgivings you might have about your ability to write, you—and indeed all writers—need to feel a connection, a motivating purpose to write compelling prose.

Select a topic that fits a *why* you care about or else you simply won't be motivated to write and consequentially, what you produce will show your apathy.

Keep in mind, the type of book we are discussing is likely to be a guide or business-related book, aimed at a specific niche in which you resonate and have expertise. While much of what we learn here can be applied to a fiction book, the benefits of writing and publishing fiction are different from those that motivate writing and publishing non-fiction.

This list of benefits to being a published author may spark an idea. Consider whether any of these fit your *why*:

PERSONAL BRANDING

A book is like an ad for your personal brand — but it doesn't look like or read like an ad. It's not an enhanced resume. Rather, it will, through anecdotes and experience, tell the reader a great deal about you as a person, in an entertaining fashion. A book allows the reader to accept what might be part of an ad or your resume with trust and no expectation of being sold a bill of goods.

Authority

When people see you as a published author of a book, you get instant credibility and authority. Only experts publish books. As a published author, you are perceived as an expert.

It's Content Marketing

Every digital marketer knows that one of the best ways in digital marketing to attract traffic is content marketing. A book is nothing but content.

No One Throws Away a Book

When you go to a networking event and give out business cards or brochures, they usually find their way to the trash (I am sure you, too, have thrown away stuff like that!). A book is never thrown away. When you give a book to someone with whom you want to do business, the book stays with them permanently. It's like re-marketing at no cost!

Speaking Opportunities

A book can help you get speaking engagements. It is solid proof that you are an expert on a subject. Book sales can provide income for speaking gigs that pay poorly or not at all. Many speakers who are authors come away from a speaking engagement with much more than the speaking fees.

A Book as a Business Card Book

Books used to market yourself need not be a big, thick tomes but they are not the size of a business card, either. It is will be a real paperback book with a spine that shows a title for visibility on a bookshelf. It's called a business-card book because the content is typically going to showcase the author professionally and not be intense or deeply thought-provoking. This type of book is also affordable for the author since they typically cost less than $1 to print.

Business Negotiations and Introductions

A book is an icebreaker. Send an autographed copy of your book to someone with whom you are about to do business. It's a gesture of confidence in yourself and your proposed project and makes the negotiations easier.

Get Your Dream Job

Companies look to hire experts. If you are an author, it's a clear signal that you know your field. Your chances of getting your dream job go up dramatically when you are an author.

Get Into Ivy League Universities

OK, so maybe this one is a little far-fetched, but identifying benefits by thinking outside of the box is good! Universities look for intelligent people. How many business schools and universities receive applications with a book? Imagine the possibilities!

Press and Media Come Looking for You

Reporters are always searching for comments and citations from experts. In today's information-centric world, who are perceived as experts? Authors!

Typically, press and media coverage is elusive and downright frustrating to get. When you are an author, an expert in the field they want, they come looking for you. And even if they don't need your expert validation for today's story, it's still easy to make important PR and media connections when you have a book published.

A Great Investment

Publishing a good book costs time and money. It is the best investment you can make in your personal brand and your company. It increases your earning potential and opens the doors to new opportunities.

Myths and Truths about Writing and Publishing a Book

I Am Not Qualified to Write a Book

Truth is that anyone can write a book. You need not be an expert to write a book. In the process of writing the book, you will in fact become an expert, and once it's published, your expertise is validated.

I NEED TO GET A PUBLISHER AND HAVE TO DEAL WITH AGENTS

Truth is that authors are no longer dependent on being discovered by an agent or in a publisher's slush pile. Technology has thrown open the doors to publishing and you do not need to contract with a publishing house. Self-publishing and digital printing have fully arrived. For a nonfiction book, it is arguably better to self-publish than go with a traditional publisher.

IT COSTS A LOT OF MONEY TO PUBLISH A BOOK

Truth is that yes, it does. It is possible to publish a book and market it with a shoestring budget of $1,000 or less. Self-publishing is common today and there are plenty of support services. However, a more realistic cost for someone who is not doing the writing or the publishing is somewhere between $3,000 and $10,000. A broad range, I know. Total costs depend on the level of support you need to pay for and how much you can do yourself.

A point to keep in mind is that in the traditional publishing house model, the publisher fronts all costs and assumes the risk that sales will recoup investment and lead to profit. In general, it is the author who sees the least share of any profit in this type of publishing, hence the popularity of self-publishing where the writer assumes the risk and reaps the reward.

IT TAKES A LONG TIME TO WRITE A BOOK. I MAY HAVE TO QUIT MY JOB AND WORK ON IT FOR MONTHS OR YEARS

Not true (although it choose to make it true). There is a chapter in this book titled *How to Write a Book in Two Weeks*. Read it. The title is not a come-on. It's a real system, a process you can follow to finish writing a book in forty hours.

The most difficult part about writing a book, aside from starting it, is often overcoming your self-doubt and fears. Once you've written a book, even if you choose not to publish it, self-doubt is no longer a factor. Cliché time, it's like riding a bike. Once you learn, even if it's been 40 years since you last hopped on a bike seat, you can in a matter of minutes be a competent rider again.

MY BOOK HAS TO BE PERFECT, IT HAS TO BE 500 PAGES WITHOUT A SINGLE MISTAKE. THE CONTENT HAS TO BE REVOLUTIONARY.

This is both a fabulous truth and a total fallacy. Change the world with your book. Awesome! Go for it.

Many of us, in truth most of us, write a book to enhance our brand and be recognized as experts. Both are valid reasons to write and publish a book. If you wait for it to be perfect, you may never publish, and for you, the myth may become reality. Don't wait.

Only a few decades ago, publishing was dramatically different. Before technology made it possible to self-publish in quantities as small as one, every book had to be perfect before it was printed. The cost to reprint was simply prohibitive.

This is no longer the reality in publishing. There is no reason to hold off on publishing to wait for perfection. Do not try to publish a perfect book — you will never end up finishing it. Publish a book and then make it perfect — it is easier that way.

Is this the best model for publishing quality books? Perhaps not, but it is the reality of publishing today.

That said, it's important to arrive as close to perfection as YOU are able to make it. When your manuscript rolls off the printing press, that first book with your name on the cover, make it as perfect as you are able. You can fix any minor transgressions before the second book rolls off the press, so don't wait for perfection to choose your life-passion and turn purpose into author-ity.

Skills, Knowledge, and Abilities

CHAPTER 4

Choose a Happiness Attitude

"The road to happiness lies in two simple principles: find what it is that Interests you and that you can do well; and when you find it, put your whole soul into it, every bit of energy and ambition and natural ability you have."

—John D. Rockefeller, III

Why is it that we always seem to want those things we don't have? And we're completely convinced that if only we had precisely that thing we want so badly, we would truly be happy?

Let me tell you about Anna, a woman who struggled with being seriously overweight for most of her adult life.

Anna

For years, Anna yo-yoed up and down the weight scale, trying every diet and weight-loss program imaginable. Eventually, she found a program that worked for her; she lost more than 100 pounds and kept the weight off. Then an odd thing happened. Anna, a person who had never suffered from mental illness, became profoundly depressed. As it turned out, Anna had focused her energies for so many years on getting thin that she warped her belief structure.

Anna's confused belief was that losing weight would solve all of her problems. She came to believe that weight loss would be a panacea, a

> miracle cure that would turn her life into a utopia. When weight loss became reality and Anna's expectation for happiness did not also become real, the true weight of her life problems hit her hard.
>
> The expectation that only certain things can make you happy will surely keep happiness out of your reach. Anna learned this the hard way.

Today, Anna has regained some weight, yet she remains much thinner than ever in her adult life. She maintains a weight that is comfortable for her. Most importantly, she has changed her attitude about what brings happiness into her life and no longer confuses her bodily image with her self-image. She discovered that being happy is a choice that begins within.

Purpose, Passion, Success: All about Choice

To walk a new path in life requires that you make a choice; that you decide; that you commit to knowing who you are. Of course, this in turn, requires that you first learn who you are.

Happiness is not created by outside circumstances; rather, your happiness is entirely within your control. Do you believe this to be a fact?

I believe and know it to be true. Outside circumstances can impact and influence our emotions, of course. And significant life events can and will bring about times of sadness and grief. But that's not what is being discussed here. We are talking about attitude and how you choose to live. Happiness is a state of mind that you choose to embrace and that you vigilantly protect against the challenges life tosses into your path on a regular basis.

> *Everyone Has a Passion; a Happiness Attitude Is Found as Passion Is Pursued*
>
> —Candy Zulkosky

Again, I ask, do you believe that happiness is not created by outside circumstances; rather, your happiness is entirely within your control?

Assuming something in your life must change or improve before you can be happy is backwards thinking. Being happy with who you are and with what you're doing comes first. Happiness comes with knowing your purpose and living your passions.

FOCUS: FIND A HAPPINESS ATTITUDE

At an essential level, happiness is simply a good feeling. It is an emotional response created by your own thoughts and temporarily affected by external circumstance.

Sounds simple, right? It should be, but rarely is. Happiness is an emotional state that is frequently misinterpreted and misunderstood. Being happy does not mean going through life with a false smile plastered on your face and ignoring all that is wrong in the world. It means finding that place inside where your contentment lies and bringing that easiness into focus every day.

One misinterpretation commonly made is to romanticize happiness. Beware of viewing the world through rose-colored glass. Eventually you have to face life without your glass armor. Equally dangerous is tying your happiness to the presence of a particular person in your life. This happened to Gina, a woman devoted to her family.

Gina

> *When her husband died unexpectedly, leaving her to raise six children between the ages of 6 and 17, Gina focused even more exclusively on raising her children. Gina lived through her children. She did not date. She did not pursue any interests that were hers alone. Every activity; every waking moment revolved around one or more of her children.*
>
> *Then one day she awakened to an empty home and an equally hollow soul. Her children were grown; some had married, some were pursuing careers, and her youngest daughter was still in college. Gina*

began crying and could not stop. She had no direction for her life and no idea how to find one.

Gina was miserably unhappy. To Gina, happiness depended on having children to care for. Gina had lived a life filled with a purpose, and a purpose she treasured, but in all that time there was no balance.

For many years, Gina had counted on external sources to define who she was. She no longer knew how to be happy alone with herself. In the end, Gina's happy face fooled no one but herself. Hiding from yourself can do great harm over time.

Fortunately for Gina, she had raised to adulthood six insightful and loving children who provided support and encouragement while she learned to stop crying and to create happiness in her life.

Today, Gina continues to guide young children. She came to understand that guiding young children was a life-passion for her, and she made it a happy purpose by becoming an advocate in the struggle against child abuse. After her youngest left for college, Gina turned her large, roomy home into a safe house for abused women and children. Gina cries now with compassion, not self-pity.

What Gina did, any one of us can do. With sure knowledge and heartfelt understanding about yourself and the part your life-passions play in your world, happiness can be yours; conditions in your life cannot help but improve.

Easily the most frequent misinterpretation of happiness is tying your happiness to some outside event, like a wedding or birth. Events like these tend to generate a state of emotional pleasure, which brings good feelings for a brief time. When such happiness comes from outside events, what you really feel is gratification, or pleasure. It's a short-term feeling of intense satisfaction.

Everyone experiences this kind of happiness, as well we should. It is fleeting by nature and does not last; it's not supposed to last. It is pleasurable and enjoyable for the moment yet has little or no long-term effect on how you approach life or on your attitude toward happiness. Events can provide you with gratification and, when continued for extended periods of time—as in Gina's case, can masquerade as happiness. Events do not impact your choice to embrace happiness as an attitude.

This bears repeating: *you have a choice to embrace happiness as an attitude.*

If you feel that you could never be happy with things the way they are in your life, you are most certainly right. Making no choice is the same as choosing to be unhappy. And both will hold you back in more ways than one. Being happy is a choice. Once you commit to being happy, once you embrace happiness as an attitude, your thoughts and actions reflect that choice. And in a cause-and-effect manner, when you choose *happy*, improvement is immediate.

There is also a pleasing side effect to happiness as an attitude. This choice inevitably moves you in the direction of your life-passions, your most treasured values and desires.

Sounds simplistic, doesn't it? It is not. There are times in life when happiness is downright impossible to embrace. Expecting happiness in the midst of grief is unrealistic and naive. Looking for happiness in the midst of world tragedy is at the least disrespectful. But it is not naive or unrealistic or simplistic or disrespectful to choose happiness, even when your world is filled with difficulty. By choosing to be genuinely happy with yourself you also choose to be the best, the strongest, the most effective person you can be. The internal strength that comes from embracing a happiness attitude will carry you through the tough times and enrich the bounty in good times.

Happiness as an Attitude

Choice affects happiness in a big way because attitude determines whether we are happy or not. Happiness as an attitude provides a feeling of well-being that can range from contentment to ecstasy. Happiness as an attitude is more than feeling giddy or giggly. It's a sense of worth found in the secure knowledge and acceptance of your true self. If you want to be happy, choose to be.

I'm not suggesting that achieving an attitude of happiness is a cure-all. We do not live in a Pollyanna world. Every day we fight years of negative conditioning. Our very language places the blame for our emotional state on external forces. How often do you say things like, *He made me mad*, or *That book depressed me*.

When you are in a situation that is generating feelings of unhappiness, change your thoughts about the situation. Will changing your point of view or changing your thought make you happy? Depends on the situation. At the very least, changing the way you view the situation will strengthen you and your response.

Adopting an attitude of happiness does not mean that you avoid emotion or ignore problems. Life happens and you must deal with it. What I am saying is that you can choose your emotional response to any situation. It's not about denying the gravity of a situation. It's about choosing how you respond, choosing the strength of an upbeat attitude in spite of the situation.

Finding your life-passion is connected to knowing who you are. Adopting an attitude of happiness in your approach to life is important to understanding who you are and is an important step in the process of finding your life-passions.

Embrace a Happiness Attitude

Choosing to embrace happiness as an attitude is a critical step along the path toward turning your life-passion into a fulfilling purpose. It's like a grapevine wreath—happiness, passion, and success are intertwined, sometimes branching off in odd directions, yet always following the same path, ultimately closing the circle.

I am an optimistic person by nature. History has proven that I am more naive and trusting in the goodness of my fellow man than is good for me. But I would not change this part of my nature for any reason and I resent heartily every ounce of regret and suspicion that has crept in through time and experience.

My ability to choose a happy attitude, to choose to see the glass as half full rather than half empty is a strength that I depend on. Over the years I have learned to temper my natural ebullience with a slight dose of paranoia, simply because the world is not a safe place. Yet you cannot convince me that man is inherently evil.

You cannot convince me that I won't succeed if I am true to my life-passion. I believe in my passions, and I believe in your ability to take your own journey to success by following your life-passions.

If you intend to succeed while following your life-passion, you will need to develop internal strength—the strength that comes from choosing happiness in your day-to-day interactions with the world. You will not succeed without it.

FOCUS: PRACTICING AN ATTITUDE OF HAPPINESS

Changing an attitude or even improving an attitude takes daily effort. A good habit that you can develop to help you maintain an attitude of happiness is to create a gratitude journal. Review your gratitude list every day. Make recording in and reviewing your gratitude journal a habit.

If gratitude does not feel comfortable to you, make it a devotional journal, or a prayer journal. If you are someone who uses affirmations, write your daily affirmations here. Or simply a few lines of positive thoughts. There's no right or wrong here. Gratitude journal is a useful name and fits for most people. The key is to reinforce the attitude of happiness you strive to create by the use of a short, daily journal exercise.

If you are a daily computer user, put this journal in a word processor or journal software of your choice and review it daily. Put a shortcut leading to your journal file on your desktop to make it easily accessible.

I use one of the writing programs I have open every day (Scribe). I have a separate Scribe notebook that I use throughout the day to record positive thoughts and affirmations that come my way.

Regardless of how you choose to use the gratitude journal, the goal is to create a sense of gratitude for what you have, for what is working, and for what is wonderful and sweet in your life.

Within your gratitude journal, consider developing a gratitude list. This will be short statements, no more than three to five. To boost the power of a gratitude list, write it out fresh daily. The act of writing, even if you are copying yesterday's list, internalizes the message and adds power to the self-communication. A daily, weekly, or even monthly gratitude list, written and read repeatedly, reminds you of why you choose a happiness attitude and makes it easier to continue making that choice in the face of a negative world.

A word about using a computer for your gratitude list. Writing in your journal on a computer is fine, especially if you are someone who is comfortable in the digital medium. However, when it comes to writing out your list, write it in pen in a notebook. Copy the list every day, adding and removing items as appropriate. We are visceral creatures. Our emotions are connected externally and internally. The act of writing is physical and spiritual. While you are writing, you are seeing the words appear. While you are writing, you are also hearing the words in your mind. This simple act of affirming your gratitude using pen and paper becomes a powerful connection, both physically and spiritually.

Take Care of Yourself

Another task that can help you to practice making happiness an attitude is to take time for yourself. Do it every day. Identify the small things in life that make you feel good and do them every day.

This task is one with which I struggle. I have learned the hard way that I must take time out, every day. For me It might be just ten minutes to enjoy a hot cup of tea and call my mother to say hello. It might be taking a few minutes to give one of the cats a little extra attention.

It might be a browse through a used bookstore or simply stopping my work long enough to watch and appreciate the sunset. It might be splurging on fresh flowers to brighten a dreary day. It is all too easy for me to fill my entire day without even once stopping to enjoy my own company.

Do something for yourself every day. Everything that reminds you that you are important and worthy will improve your outlook on life.

When you are practicing a happiness attitude, it helps to be reminded of positive thoughts and positive attitudes. Become an inspiration collector. Get a book of positive, inspirational thoughts and keep it where you can read one or two thoughts each day. Everyone can make time to read at least one positive message daily. There are websites and blogs that offer nothing but inspirational slogans every day and include colorful and fun images, too.

Record a positive message in your gratitude journal. Do this daily, if you can. At the very least, do not let more than a week go by without recording a positive message in your gratitude journal.

Your positive message is likely to come from something you read. But don't overlook the possibility of finding positive messages in your own writing, in what you hear others say, in life lessons you might have learned this day, or in normal everyday inspiring experiences.

Make these three activities a habit. Being an inspiration collector, doing something—no matter how small—for yourself daily, and keeping your gratitude journal take very little time. Yet from this tiny time commitment comes tremendous attitude wealth.

Happiness and Your Life-Passion

It is up to us to guard against unhappiness. Fortunately, there are activities and methods to follow that help make the choice of happiness easier to embrace.

Have you ever wondered why people jog? I've tried it and I don't get it, most likely because I simply don't like to run. Put me in a pool of water, however, and you can't get me out. Swimming is an activity that gives me pleasure. I am happy when I swim. I remain in a good mood for a long time after swimming is done. I am refreshed and energized.

Moving our bodies generates endorphins, feel-good hormones. For some, this happens with running. What kind of movement gives you that feel-good sensation?

Choosing to exercise or move a little every day helps you to create and maintain a happiness attitude. You don't have to swim or jog. Your exercise can be as simple as walking down to the end of the block to mail your letters instead of leaving them in your box for the letter carrier to collect.

By the way, the benefit of physical activity is boosted when your activity of choice involves being outside. As I write this, I am seated on my patio enjoying a pleasant breeze, sunshine, and playful kittens. Granted, writing is not especially physical, but nature rejuvenates and restores the human spirit. When exercise is combined with nature, it has a powerful kick. Whatever your brand of exercise, whether it be in or out of nature, give yourself the gift of visiting it frequently. Move your body toward a happiness attitude.

Are you a creative person? Susan, one of my very best friends, claims she has no creative bones in her body. I know she's wrong because everyone is creative. It is just that some people find more pleasure in the creative process than others; hence they enjoy more feel-good feedback from the experience.

Being creative is a feel-good task. Creativity and self-expression are internal happiness generators. Staying in touch with your creative side is an important part of approaching your life with a healthy attitude of happiness.

Being creative does not have to mean writing or creating art. My friend Susan, who believes she is not creative, glows with creativity when she is planning an event, or arguing a point of logic, or taking care of her sweetheart. Your creativity might be growing flowers, or being an especially good cook, or fixing cars. The creativity muscle, like any other muscle, must be worked regularly to remain healthy. Schedule creative time each day, even if it's only a few minutes.

You cannot change the 'what' of your life without changing the 'who' of your life. Change how you think, change how you believe, change how you respond to the world—make happiness a choice.

Do you think that I set an easy task by asking you to embrace a happiness attitude in your life? Changing beliefs is hard work. Yet, what of the alternative? It is harder to continually lie to yourself. It is harder to live a life filled with frustration and depression. The key is to change what you have control of (yourself) and let go of the rest.

Change your point of view. Get in touch with nature. Become uniquely creative. Get active every day. Attitude follows thought and thought follows action.

Take a moment and do a visualization. Think about something—perhaps an event—that would make you happy. It may be getting a big promotion at work, closing a tough client, meeting Mr. Right, or getting an unexpected financial windfall. Visualize yourself attaining all of your goals and dreams. Close your eyes and picture it vividly.

How did it feel? You're probably feeling happy right now. It's a good feeling, isn't it?

Yes. Happiness is a good feeling. It is your own thoughts that create the emotion we call happiness. You just proved that. Whatever you visualized was not actually happening right then, yet you felt the emotion of happiness. And by the way, you also proved that you are capable of making the choice to be happy. Happiness is an attitude, and choice affects attitude in a big way.

What about your life today makes you happy? What is missing now from your life that would make you happy if it were in your life?

Achieving an attitude of happiness may come naturally to you if you are an optimist by natural inclination. I've found, however, that even those of us who tend to be positive and upbeat still have to work at maintaining a happy attitude.

Today's world does not make happiness easy, yet it is exactly because of the state of our ever-shrinking world that we must each do what is in our power to help. And it is in your power, in my power, in the power of every single being to make this small, individual change. Adopt an attitude of happiness.

Here's a challenge for you: for one entire day, be happy.

When something happens that would normally cause you to react with anger or to become unhappy, change your choice. Really look at your own thoughts. It's not necessary to deny irritation or unhappiness if you don't like a situation, simply choose to find a way to be positive in spite of that situation.

It takes practice, but you can choose happiness! Remember not to ignore feelings; rather, question the cause of your anger or impatience. If you are in a situation where you must embrace the emotion, then at least make that a conscious choice. Try instead to think of something pleasant, maybe something on your gratitude list, which will help you to focus on being happy.

If you want to feel differently, you can. Try happiness for a day. Start with an hour then add in the next hour. It might grow on you.

Look and Learn from Past Lessons

CHAPTER 5

Seek and You Shall Find

"One of my greatest fears is not being able to change, to be caught in a never-ending cycle of sameness. Growth is so important."

—Matt Dillon

Why is it that so many of us—perhaps you included—know what to do, have the desire to do it, yet do not follow through? Is it fear? Apathy? Anger? Doubt? Uncertainty? All of these emotions can and do cause a mental lock down. Quite simply, we are experts at convincing ourselves that it is easier to keep on doing what we've always done, even when we know that what we've always done no longer works!

If we do not look at our past and the lessons we've learned there, we will continue to repeat the same past over and over. How can the situation improve if your current life is a mirror of your past life?

FOCUS: SEARCH YOUR PAST; TELESCOPE TO YOUR FUTURE

The definition of insanity is repeating the same actions and expecting a different result (another cliché of which I'm fond). If your past and your now both exclude active involvement with your life-passions, then the cliché is proven true. This is truly an insane way to walk the journey of your life.

Look to your past to find your future. Step through your fears. Embrace needed changes. Learn to fully experience your life-passions.

Looking to your past to find your future means learning from your past actions in order to design a future built on those lessons.

Challenges and How You Respond

*C*ircle of Sameness. I did not invent this particular meme, but I've not found a more descriptive term for continuing to repeat the same mistakes over and over and over again. How do you address problems, especially those that reoccur?

Are you one of the many who routinely makes a wrong turn into the circle of sameness? This circle is a self-defeating attitude that feeds on fear and the unfinished business in your past.

Ideally, each of us looks to our past to find our future, learn from the experience, and embrace change. Responding to life with positive, healthy, and growth-enabling actions is a worthy goal and ensures that the circle of sameness becomes open-ended.

Most people are designed to repeat their failures, to repeat what they've already proven that they can do. Getting stuck in the circle of sameness makes it convenient to come up with reasons for why your life is not what it could be. Getting stuck is unbelievably easy and happens to all of us.

Staying stuck is a different matter.

When it comes to evaluating our past actions, each of us had at least two paths to choose from before we acted. If you are filled with frustration, with disappointment, are tired and bored—then your choice was likely the path leading to the circle of sameness.

If you are confident, in control, filled with creative energy, and directed—then you will not be trapped in the circle of sameness. Rather, you learn from past experiences. You use knowledge and self-evaluation to make effective choices and take appropriate actions.

FOCUS: SEARCH OUT LIFE'S CHALLENGES

What can you do to ensure that you choose the path to growth?

There are five simple questions that can be applied to any challenge, difficulty, problem, situation, or conflict (choose your own descriptor, these questions are not situational dependent).

When you are faced with a difficult situation or a counterproductive environment, simply stop and find an answer to each of these questions before you act and you will always take the path to growth:

1. Can I influence the situation?
2. Do I want to change the situation?
3. Do I have the power to change the situation?
4. Can I eliminate the problem?
5. Can I accept the current situation?

Think about it. If you have the power to influence the situation, then you can use that influence for positive change and eliminate the problem.

If you answer no to the first three questions, then you have only two choices. Either live with the situation or get out.

By taking time out to consider what is in your power to achieve, you open doors that otherwise would not even be visible to you and enable choices that might not have been possible.

FOCUS: LOOK AND LEARN FROM YOUR PAST

The first rung on the ladder—and on every other step taken—is you. Give yourself every benefit and opportunity to grow.

It's important to clarify your attitude toward the events, problems, and challenges of daily life. These are the actions that determine the path your life follows.

Do you choose the circle of sameness or the road to growth?

Choose Your Path

The graphic demonstrates the choice and resulting actions each of us face hundreds of times daily without even being aware of it. When you react to life, you choose the path leading to sameness. When you respond to life, you choose the path to growth.

React is about speed and emotion. Reacting is acting without using your brain to think first; it's reflexive and instinctive. Reacting leads to crisis, not solution. Reaction leads to cleaning up messes—yours and others. Reaction leads to blame. Rarely do we accept that the blame is attached to ourselves. Reaction leads to punishment. Worst of all, reaction repeats the circle with no lesson learned and no growth.

Sadly, reaction stifles everyone—neither you or the persons you are reacting to are able to grow when you react. Think of it this way: when you react, you open your mouth and insert your foot.

Respond is about thought. It's about taking a step back to consider the consequences to you and others before you act. Respond can also be about speed, but never at the expense of consideration. Respond is about dealing with people, not creating problems or crisis. Respond is about having options and making choices instead of cleaning up messes.

Respond is about implementing solutions, not dealing out blame and punishment.

Respond is about learning from your actions and building a base for future success. When you respond, you open your mouth and close it again before your foot gets there.

Will you always respond rather than react? No. There will always be drama and times when we react. For instance, I am by nature calm and likely to respond in any given situation. Yet, I also have what I call a fairness button. When I face injustice or what I perceive as injustice, anyone pushing this button spurs me to react.

By being clear about purpose and aware that the choice to respond is mine, I am better able to avoid reacting even when my button is pushed. The same is true for you. You have the opportunity, in any situation, to choose the path toward growth instead of sameness by being aware, by choosing to respond instead of react.

Which path do you choose?

Are you more likely to react or respond when faced with a surprising circumstance? Think about events or situations that have occurred in your life recently. Perhaps a crisis at work, a problem with your children, or your spouse, how you handled the neighbor's barking dog, the jerk at the red light who cut you off.

If you reacted in any of these situations, would you choose to act differently now that you've had time to consider? Do you think that the outcome of a situation to which you reacted would have been more satisfying or more successful had you stepped back a moment and chosen to respond instead?

Your choice in any situation is to react or respond. Your choice is to remain the same or grow. The consequences of your choice may prove one choice to be better than the other and one of your choices may lead to a more successful outcome than another, but neither choice is wrong.

Explore Personal Characteristics and Balance

Chapter 6

The Dynamic You

"One must have the adventurous daring to accept oneself as a bundle of possibilities and undertake the most interesting game in the world—making the most of one's best."

—Harry Emerson Fosdick

Putting your life-passion to work for you means learning how to build a future that makes you smile in your public life as well as your private life. It also means learning to become a more dynamic you.

Have you ever known someone whom you could describe as dynamic? We most often use dynamic to describe a person who is especially vibrant, vigorous, or intense. Dynamic people are governed by the same characteristics as dynamic actions.

Dynamic is an interesting word; it's a word that has many meanings and is a strong word of action. One dictionary defines dynamic as *actions characterized by continuous change, activity, or progress*. In the computer world, the definition of dynamic is taken a step further to mean *actions that make changes to other actions without additional commands*. The commonality between these definitions is action. To be more precise, it's action that includes activity, change, and progress.

The word dynamic, no matter whom or what it is describing, always indicates that a give-and-take, an interaction, is taking place.

When the give-and-take is you interacting with yourself, that dynamic you blooms into someone powerful and vibrant. You become a force for creating continuous change and making interactive progress within yourself.

Shake Hands with the Dynamic You

It's like rolling a small snowball down a snowy slope. When you get in touch with the dynamic you, internal changes are set in motion. When you get in touch with the dynamic you, one action leads to another with little additional effort on your part.

The dynamic you is a force for change. The dynamic you has energy and drive. The dynamic you is in motion, always changing yet staying the same. The dynamic you is marked by a vigor and intensity that has, perhaps, not been the normal experience for you.

Choose to be dynamic. Choose to get in touch with the dynamic you. Begin by defining who you are, what your natural traits and behaviors are, and what your beliefs and attitudes are. Begin by understanding your strengths and your limitations.

It's time to pound your chest and tell the world how great and unique you are. If you want an exercise to help you get in touch with your uniqueness, then write a story about the dynamic you. It's not necessary to show the story to anyone else, although you can, of course. Don't get hung up on structure or grammar or spelling. It's an exercise, and as such it is necessary that you brag on yourself and focus on what the world needs that you have to give.

Beliefs, Attitudes, and Behaviors

Let's talk about limitations, about roadblocks. You benefit in direct proportion to your effort. Regardless of my efforts to create meaningful content and provide avenues for growth, the role that my effort plays in your success has less than ten percent to do with the benefits you experience.

Are there roadblocks you will throw up to sabotage your success? Yes. I don't know what they might be, but I know that they will exist. It is an odd truth that we are perfectly designed for exactly the life and success we currently enjoy.

Beware of self-sabotage. It is insidious, sneaky, and downright depressing. It is difficult to self-diagnose—but it's not impossible.

Beliefs, attitudes, and behaviors are what define our actions. And regardless of what you might think you want, actions speak the truth of your beliefs.

Look closely at your beliefs and attitudes and the behaviors that result. If the behavior leads to a less than satisfactory result, then backtrack to the attitude and belief that cause the behavior.

I'll bet that you've said, or heard someone else say, "bad things always happen to me" or "I'm always lucky." What we say echoes what we believe and becomes a self-fulfilling prophecy.

Gary Barnes, of Gary Barnes International, is a prominent business coach known by some as the no-try guy. Gary declares his seminars and boot camps to be a no-try zone. Every time the word *try* is used, the attendees are asked to make the sound of a buzzer to bring the use of try to the user and everyone else's attention. This is amazingly annoying and effective.

Eliminate try. Do instead. It will surprise you to discover how often we hedge our bets, verbally. And every time, we are reinforcing our beliefs. It will also surprise you to recognize how many times a day we use hedge words like try. Go ahead. I challenge you. Spend a day without try, without waffling and hedging.

FOCUS: EXPLORE POWER AND PURPOSE IN YOUR BELIEFS

Positive. Negative. Good. Bad. Pure. Evil. Yin. Yang.

Each of us has a core set of beliefs that underlie and define our values. I believe that these values, in themselves are inherently non-judgmental. There is no good or bad associated with our core beliefs. It's how we codify and corrupt these beliefs that attaches a negative, or even a positive, connotation.

Most of us do not consciously decide what we're going to believe. We interpret past events, follow the lead of others, and are influenced by painful and pleasurable experiences. Beliefs are feelings, which we understand and interpret from our own unique perspective. When a feeling becomes a certainty, when you define a feeling as a certainty and apply meaning—with or without concrete proof—that is a belief.

How do ideas turn into beliefs? Tony Robbins shares an example when he says, "Think of an idea like a tabletop with no legs. Without any legs, the tabletop won't even stand up by itself. Belief, on the other hand, has legs. To believe something, you have references to support the idea—specific experiences that back up the belief. These are the legs that make your tabletop solid and that make you certain about your beliefs. For example, if you believe you're extremely intelligent, you likely have a lot of references to back it up."

What is important is to be aware of your beliefs—those you hold currently, those you are creating now, those you might want to create. Beliefs, once understood and acknowledged by you, are empowering.

Are your beliefs providing support to move you in the direction you want to go? If not, change them. When your certainty—when your beliefs—are powerful and positive, you can accomplish great things.

Beliefs are personal and I don't presume to advise you as to what you should believe. Here are a few of my favorite empowering beliefs. Feel free to adopt any that ring true for you.

- There is always a way if I'm committed.
- There are no failures—as long as I am learning, I'm succeeding.
- Everything happens for a reason and a purpose that serves me.
- I find great joy in little things… a smile… a flower… a sunset.

- I give more of myself to others than anyone expects.
- I create my own reality and am responsible for what I create.
- If I'm confused, I'm about to learn something.
- Every day above ground is a great day.

When we speak in negative terms, then the belief our words reinforce is that events are beyond our control, that events just happen. When we expect the worst and don't accept responsibility for our actions or our relationships, then guess what? We get exactly what we believe and expect.

Your beliefs state what you think to be true, regardless of whether or not you have actual proof to support your belief. It is important to examine your beliefs from time to time to be sure that they are accurate and helpful, not restricting your actions.

Why do you behave the way you do? Why do you do what you do? Why do you act the way you act? Why do you feel the way you feel? Because of your beliefs.

Why are people so different? Why do some people do better at certain jobs than others? Is it because their behaviors are influenced by their innate attitudes and values? Yes, it is.

This book is not about techniques. It is about how to be. And how to be comes from inside you. Beliefs are the windows to your world, to your perception of reality. Beliefs control attitude, altitude, and behavior.

- Are you a natural leader who desires power and wants to influence people?
- Do you have a desire to achieve wealth?
- Is your interest in the pursuit of truth and knowledge in a systematized fashion?
- Are your values traditional when it comes to such things as religion or authority and the defined rules and principles of living?

- Do you just love to be around people?
- Are you kind, sympathetic, and unselfish?
- Are you interested in form and harmony? Is your primary interest in the artistic episodes of life?

There are no right or wrong answers to these questions. Your answers, however, can define beliefs. Belief is a perception of reality that you accept as true. Belief is, in fact, a perception that your mind has proven to be true. Once the perception becomes belief, everything you see and do is designed to prove the belief.

An attitude is a mental position, a feeling or an emotional response to your environment that causes you to value certain experiences, people, and activities and causes you to devalue others. Attitudes are the ideas, principles, standards, and causes that are important to you. They are your reason for behaving in one way and not another.

Where does self, purpose, and being a dynamic you fall in this equation of belief, attitude, and behavior?

When it comes to the concept of self, we all have a bit of Sybil in us. We each have multiple personalities of self. For instance, self-confidence and self-esteem are commonly defined as how you are perceived on the outside. People are cued how to act toward you by how they feel when they are around you. Your self-confidence and self-esteem both contribute to that external self.

Self-worth is considered to be you on the inside, but it's actually more. When defining self-worth, self-confidence is your inner strength, the secret you deep inside that keeps the rest of your selves intact.

Self-respect is your belief in your worth, your belief that you are worthy of the success that you desire. Self-esteem is your belief in yourself, your belief in the value of how you feel. It takes all three of these selves to create a balanced and healthy self-worth.

Self-worth is at the center of belief. Belief is your perception, attitude is your reason, and behavior is what you do to make beliefs real and justify attitudes.

FOCUS: SILVER LINING OR CLOUD?

Changing an attitude, or even improving an attitude, takes daily effort. Do you tend to be a positive thinker or a negative thinker? Do you see the glass half full or half empty? Most people are a mixture of both. And on any given day, even a positive thinker can see nothing but clouds, no matter how obvious the silver lining. Be alert to those times when your tendency is to lean toward a negative attitude. It's easier to regain balance when you are newly or only slightly shifted away from the positive.

A good exercise to repeat regularly is to write your gratitude list in a form that creates clarifying statements that reinforce beliefs. Keep in mind that the way you phrase these statements must be considered and evaluated for beliefs that might be getting in the way of you achieving your goals.

For instance, if this is something you would write, you are likely in a space most would consider good:

- I have a wonderful support system in my life.
- Everything is changeable, including my habits.
- I like myself and believe I deserve a good life.
- Now consider the next statements.
- I don't like my job, but it pays well. I'm too old to start over.
- I am a creative person.
- People often try to con me.
- Life is hard.

Do these statements accurately reflect your beliefs? If so, are these beliefs that you want to embrace?

Write and evaluate your own belief statements. If any ring false to you or reinforce actions you do not want, then reframe the belief statement. Turn it into a positive re-statement of the belief that you want in your life.

Include these belief statements as part of your gratitude list to be written out by hand every day.

By the way, if you put a 'but' in any belief or gratitude statement, take a hard look—it is likely that you are justifying a belief that you are afraid to change.

An example of reframing might be this:

Original: I want a new job, but no one will hire me because I'm over 40.

Reframed: Employers are looking for people like me who have demonstrated their reliability and skill.

It is normal and natural to have a mixture of positive and negative beliefs and attitudes. Focus on the positive is obviously preferable. Beliefs should open your eyes to opportunity and make you willing to try new ways of thinking, doing, or seeing. Beliefs that hinder you will, if they have not already, turn into roadblocks and self-fulfilling prophecies of the worst kind.

CHAPTER 7

Your Personality Strengths

"Passion is energy. Feel the power that comes from focusing on what excites you."

—Oprah Winfrey

While beliefs color your world, the form your life takes is supported by your personality strengths; sometimes referred to as your personal and occupational assets. It is through examining these personality strengths that we identify and make full use of our life-passions.

There are four essentials that comprise your personality strengths, each vital to your life-passions and, by design, to your purpose.

- Knowledge, skills, and abilities,
- Natural personality,
- Experience and experiences,
- Purpose and passion.

What you know and what you can do. Your natural tendencies. Your daily and cumulative life experience. The passion you feel and the purpose you put into your daily life. These are the sum of your personality strengths. These essentials, your personality strengths, are a unique combination of personal assets that in large measures define how others see you as well as how you believe yourself to be perceived.

Personality strengths are in constant flux, changing and evolving as you add new experiences to your life. This changeability and flexibility is one of the wonders of being human and is vitally important to healthy personal growth.

Yet, at the heart of your personality is a core strength, a solid base of beliefs and passions that does not change, rather, it serves as a foundation upon which life builds your personality—with or without your conscious input. I don't know about you, but if I have a choice between a life that happens to me or a life over which I have some control, I'll take control. Learning to understand how your personality strengths intersect and evolve allows you the power of choice.

Knowledge, Skills, and Abilities

Your personality strengths begin with knowledge. It is your answer to these questions that defines and describes your knowledge, skills, and ability assets:

> What do I know?

> What can I do?

Knowledge is what you know. It really does not matter how you learned; your knowledge is gained through experience, education, and training as well as less formal activities like reading, television, movies, or people watching.

What you can do is described by both skills and abilities. Your abilities are what you can do naturally. Abilities are enhanced by learning and honed by experience. Skills, on the other hand, are learned. You may have been born with an innate understanding of all things mechanical, but you have to learn specific skills to become an engineer or mechanic. Skill and ability are twin orbs rotating in tandem around the planet called knowledge. OK, that's a little hokey, but the image describes this yin and yang relationship.

FOCUS: STRENGTH OF KNOWLEDGE AND ABILITIES

Have you ever known someone who was book smart but couldn't find their own nose without a map, someone with no common sense or practical experience? To become skilled at any activity takes both practice and knowledge.

You have your own unique selection of skills that are pooled together in combinations that create the various skill-sets you use in the different parts of your life.

TRANSFERABLE SKILLS

Think about the skills you have that have been useful in many different situations. Skills that are transferable are especially useful because they can be used in almost any kind of work. Communication skills, leadership skills, computer skills, interpersonal skills, and thinking skills are good examples. These skills, whether learned or natural, transfer easily from one project, job, or task to another.

WORK-SPECIFIC SKILLS

Not all of the skills you develop as part of your career will be useful in all professional applications. Some work skills are specific, specialized skills needed to do particular types of work. Work-specific skills are usually learned through training—in the classroom or on the job—and through observation and practice.

Work-specific skills may be unique to a particular job, company, or industry. They must be updated or changed as the work changes and as new procedures, technologies, or processes are introduced

PERSONAL MANAGEMENT SKILLS

It takes a different set of skills to manage your life. These skills allow you to live in harmony with yourself, your work, your community, and the world in general. If you have good personal management skills, you become flexible and able to adapt easily to a variety of life situations.

For someone considering self-employment or starting a business, personal management skills become critical. Without a boss to define your work schedule and organize your occupational life, it is up to you.

If you have good personal management skills, you will find it easier to successfully transition between holding down a job and becoming an entrepreneur.

Do you have these personal management skills? Read through these descriptions and evaluate your own skills. Which of these is your strongest skill-set? Which is the weakest? Which is the easiest, most intuitive for you?

Keep in mind that skills are learned Those that come easiest are often closely attuned to your innate abilities and should not be taken for granted just because knowledge and skill comes with little effort. Even a musical prodigy must learn and then practice to maintain and focus that God-given ability.

ORGANIZATIONAL SKILL

No matter what type of work you do, the ability to work in an organized manner makes you more effective. Statistics show that people are working more hours per week than they did a decade ago.

To deal with a heavier workload, you need to be well organized, both at work and at home. This is especially true if your choice is to work at home.

MONEY MANAGEMENT SKILLS.

Effective money management skills are important for everyone. As a reader of this book, it is likely that you have a more than passing interest in becoming self-employed in some fashion.

This means you will assume greater responsibility for expenses such as health care, disability, and retirement plans than you have as a full-time employee receiving the same benefits from an employer.

Effective money management can make possible both the business and life success you want and will allow you to work the way you want. Carrying low debt and maintaining a good credit rating make it easier for you to obtain a loan, get a line of credit, lease a car or office equipment, and so on.

In turn, these assets broaden the range of work options open to you.

Time Management Skills

Having more things to do and less time to do them in is an increasingly common situation. Managing your time effectively helps you to balance the roles you play in life. It also helps you to meet project deadlines and arrive at appointments on time. If you don't happen to be talented in time management, there are countless tools and trainings available, both free and paid. Take the time to find a system that you are comfortable using so that you will in fact use it.

Time management requires setting priorities-deciding what is most important and when it needs to be accomplished. The ability to predict how much time things will take is critical to effective time management Being able to say NO is an important part of time management, too.

Self-Employed Business Skills

Whether you're currently employed, self-employed, or looking to be self-employed, it's to your advantage to view yourself as if you were a business. This will help you to understand the importance of marketing your services and skills, maintaining your effectiveness as a worker by finding creative ways to keep learning, and building working relationships and networks with others—both inside and outside your workplace.

Managing yourself as if you were a business implies that you have a clear picture of where you want to take your business and that you have business goals guiding your actions.

Health and Lifestyle-Related Skills

How well you take care of yourself can have a big impact on what you are able or willing to do. That's why eating well, exercising, and getting enough rest and relaxation is so critical. It is the bane of the home worker to find separation between work and home a challenge. It is just as easy to suffer burn-out working from a home environment as it is working in an office. Good health is required to manage stress effectively and balance the many different roles you play in life (e.g., student, parent, business owner, spouse).

There is strength and power in knowledge. One of the identifying features of a life-passion is an infusion of knowledge and skill. Strong natural abilities are also often part of a life-passion.

Identifying your skills and abilities is an important step in developing your life-passion into author-ity. Adding to your knowledge base, focusing your abilities, and expanding your skills are physical actions that can lead directly to the achievement of your dreams and goals.

The things you have learned outside the classroom, through life experience and leisure activities, are among your most important personal assets.

What Do You know?

Are you struggling to answer this question? What do you know? Don't be discouraged. Many find this kind of introspection challenging. It's useful to brainstorm a list of topics and tasks you have learned in the past five years. Review the list you come up with, then break out your knowledge, skills, and abilities into manageable bites in order to explore and come to understand how important an asset your experience can be.

Another exercise that can be helpful is to look at the list of skills and identify any that are transferrable, meaning they transfer easily from one job, project, or task to another.

According to research, the average person has more than 700 skills and tasks that they do well. Can you list 700 things that you do well? It is a challenge. If you want to boost your appreciation for what you can do, take it on.

And one more exercise that's useful in exploring your knowledge and abilities. Write out a lists of the ten skills you do best, another list of the ten skills you enjoy the most, and another list of the ten skills you would like to develop.

In my experience, you will find that you know more and can do more than you think. Most people underestimate their skills and abilities.

Personality Strength: Natural Personality

Your temperament is a combination of your nature, your disposition, and your personality. Scientists who study human development believe that each of us has a natural temperament or preference for acting or thinking a certain way.

For example, you have a preferred handedness; you are most likely either left or right handed. When you write with your preferred hand, the action feels natural, comfortable, and easy. If you sign your name with your other (non-preferred) hand, you find it an unnatural, awkward, and difficult task. Even an ambidextrous person will favor one hand over the other.

Temperament is how you approach life naturally. It's the personality that you wear easily and comfortably.

FOCUS: THE POTENCY OF YOUR NATURAL PERSONALITY

We think of temperament and personality as opposing tendencies. Consider whether one or more of these describes how you approach your daily life:

- Are you a big-picture person who is visionary, future oriented and imaginative?

- Are you a detail person who prefers to focus on one thing at a time, is oriented toward the present, and prefers to work in a step-by-step fashion?

- Are you a thinker who is able to look inward, ponder things, and find creative answers to the questions life holds?

- Are you a doer who is good at putting thought into action and getting things done?

Your natural personality will include tendencies from more than one of these approaches. Understanding which approach is strongest in you can be useful in predicting your own as well as other people's behavior.

One type of personality is not better or worse than another—your temperament cannot be right or wrong. It's simply your natural approach to life, your inclination to be a certain way. Each type of personality has its own strengths and weaknesses. We need people with all kinds of temperaments to provide balance in a healthy society. Exploring your personality characteristics in an honest and accepting way:

- Improves your ability to recognize which occupational opportunities will be best for you.

- Helps you to recognize weaknesses associated with your temperament and deliberately work to offset them. For example, if you know you tend to be a detail person, you may look for ways to develop your ability to keep the big picture in mind. You might choose to work with big-picture people or deliberately step back from your work periodically to examine the whole forest instead of individual trees.

- Enhances your interpersonal skills by gaining greater understanding of how the natural personality characteristics predict the behaviors of people around you.

Your personal characteristics describe the way you usually approach situations and how you choose to act. For example, in your everyday world, your approach or focus to a given task may include some, all, or none of these characteristics:

- Dependable and honest
- Flexible and adaptable,
- Patient,
- Optimistic,
- A risk taker.

The values you hold dearest are the basis of your personality. Widely accepted science has identified several basic values present to varying degrees in each of us. Gaining insight into these values opens a door to hidden motivators which can help you to identify the discrepancies between what you believe you want and the reality of what you have.

Tony Robbins offers a free DISC personal strengths profile. (That stands for Dominance, Influence, Steadiness, and Compliance.) (https://www.tonyrobbins.com/ue/)

It takes about fifteen minutes to fill out the DISC questionnaire online, and you get the results right away in downloadable form. And, while the Robbins organization does contact you and require that you set up a free profile on their website, they do not inundate you with email solicitations.

There are a number of different ways to learn about your personality. They don't always have to be formal, serious, or scholarly methods. Even magazine quizzes and horoscopes provide opportunities to read about personal characteristics as well as give you the opportunity to assess whether they apply to you or not. Here's a just-for-fun personality test at the QuizRocket website: http://www.quizrocket.com/fun-personality-quiz

Personality assessments can help, but keep in mind that they provide information that, while tailored to your responses, remains generic to a relatively high degree. The tests can provide valuable guidance, direction, and assistance for use in making decisions. Personality assessments cannot tell you what is right for you—only you can decide that.

Not interested in personality assessments? Another method of getting in touch with how our personalities impact our life choices can be found in our stories. How we relate life experiences and how we've dealt with life in general reveal clues about the types of people we are.

Consider Your Stories

Think of several (three to five) stories that describe events that happened in your life. These don't have to be significant, life-altering events. Rather, think of times when you did something that gave you a sense of achievement or satisfaction or a time when you made a difference in some way or to someone.

It's best to write (or transcribe an audio record) the stories, but remembering and thinking about each story is also effective.

Consider the characteristics you displayed for each story. Were you a positive thinker? A risk taker? A good manager? Curious? Responsible? Flexible? List the characteristics, using your own words, that you exhibited for each story. These are clues to the kind of person you are.

This can be taken a step further as well by identifying the knowledge, skills, and abilities you used for the experience and the tasks involved.

These and other personality traits can be helpful in identifying hidden motivators, revealing what you value and what your values are, as well as pointing out your life-passions.

What are five of your personal characteristics? Select five words that describe you. Use the list from your stories, if you made a list. Otherwise, think about five words that you believe other people would use to describe you (e.g., determined, creative, detailed).

Explore these five words. For instance, write a paragraph about yourself that uses all five words to describe you as you see and think of yourself and then again as you believe others see and think of you. If you want to take it a step further, give those five words to a friend or co-worker and ask them to write a paragraph.

Experience and Experiences

When evaluating personality strengths, there is another extremely important category to consider: your experience and experiences. These comprise one of our most valued resources. Yet, self-help gurus often overlook them.

Experience and experiences are the wealth and riches of your personal strengths—the assets that can determine whether or not your dreams are within your reach. By definition, these assets are unique to you. No one else will have the same history as yours which makes you uniquely suited to a variety of occupational choices.

Which occupation is right for you? Pursuing a career in management? Owning a retail store? Becoming a freelance technical writer or editor? Tooling your computer skills into a web-based income? The answer best suited to your unique strengths will become clearer as we explore the undervalued clout of your personal experience and experiences.

What are your unique life experiences?

Have you ever experienced that party game where one person whispers a phrase to another and it's whispered in sequence to several (or many) others, then at the end it's spoken aloud by the last person in the chain and bears little resemblance to what was actually said at the start? It's hilarious and a real example of how a group of people can share the same experience yet have a unique experience.

You have a unique perspective on the world and how you interact and have interacted with it. Capture your uniqueness and fold it into the dynamic you.

Do you know which are your most important resources? It's difficult to simply list your most important resources because their relevance often depends on the occupation you are considering. If you intend to start a business selling soccer uniforms, then experience coaching your daughter's soccer team would be a definite asset. But that same experience may be of little value if your dream is to open up a wedding boutique.

FOCUS: THE UNDERVALUED CLOUT OF YOUR EXPERIENCE

Each one of us follows a unique life path, a trek that is molded by and depends upon our experiences. No one else has the same combination of life experiences you do.

For some, that life trek will be extraordinary. For the vast majority, it will be something less than extraordinary, but still amazing. It is important to know that it is not necessary to be a champion.

Yes, to excel is a great accomplishment and a worthy objective, but take care not to overlook the value of less dramatic accomplishments like caring for an ailing parent or helping a child chart the stars for a science project because you've always had a secret passion for astronomy.

Keep in mind, too, that it is not always the positive experience that molds us. We learn as much if not more from the dark or sad parts of our personal history.

Experiences such as recovering from substance abuse, surviving the unexpected, loss of employment, or learning to cope with illness can give you wisdom and compassion that others who have not had these life experiences won't have.

Our experience also provides knowledge of the systems and processes that are needed to resolve those life challenges. Experience is of value to you, both those experiences found in your personal life and those found in your work life.

Do you have experience in education or training?

I'm a big believer in never-ending learning. Even if you are not a trainer or teacher, you are a seeker of knowledge and can draw upon (and share) what you have learned to fuel the dynamic you. This might include formal education, training, or conferences, but don't sell your experiences in the schools of life short.

WHAT ARE THE SUPPORT SYSTEMS YOU DEPEND ON?

When I first started, years ago, as a freelancer writing features for a regional newspaper, the people, clubs, organizations, and connections that I depended on to help me grow as a writer and perform as a reporter were completely different from those I count on today. As the topics and type of writing I do change, so does my sphere of influence for both those I impact and those who have an impact on me.

Ask yourself, what are the support systems in your life today that will assist you in achieving your goals? Your dreams? To become a dynamic you? To balance your activities? Make sure that you have the right set of tools to support whatever your objectives are because those tools change as we change and it's important to have an effective toolbox of support systems to draw upon.

No matter how independent and self-sufficient you are, the reality is that we all could use a little help now and then. We are particularly in need of support when our lives are changing significantly. Perhaps your life is in flux, or you want it to be different. You will especially benefit at a time of great potential change from your supportive systems. The more sources of support and information you know and use, the better. Your support may come from:

PERSONAL SOURCES SUCH AS FRIENDS AND FAMILY.

Professional sources such as colleagues, classmates, instructors, and employers. Also community resources such as counselors, religious leaders, and staff in libraries and career centers.

When you are making a transition—be it work, education, or a business start-up— building a support system is an important factor in making the transition a success. You should have many support systems, many clusters of people who can be helpful to you. Relying on one person to provide all the support you need during a time of transition can put a great deal of strain on your relationship.

It is likely that your major support systems already exist. However, if that's not the case, or if you simply feel the need to boost your support system, you can build effective support systems with a surprisingly small effort.

Here are some possibilities:

- Identify the types of information and support you need (financial, educational, emotional).
- List your current supports and resources.
- Figure out where you can get more of the types of support you need.

Are you overlooking material & financial resources?

A few years ago my stepmother passed away and my father and I discussed when he would come to live with me. At that time, he chose to stay in his home for a while longer and agreed that he would begin to downsize. Two years later when it became medically necessary for him to come live with me, I was grateful for the effort he had put into divesting himself of my stepmother's possessions and many of his own. He understood the need to take only those assets that would be beneficial to the next step in his evolution.

We do, indeed, live in a material world. You have assets that are not necessarily financial yet have value. Consider what you might use in your evolution into a dynamic you. I can't say what items you own or to which you have access that could be of value in this way; you'll need to make that assessment.

Many people fail to consider material resources when reviewing personal assets. Your material resources can give you options that may not be open to others.

Material resources are not necessarily financial ones. For example, owning your own computer allows you to work out of your home. If you want to be self-employed, being on the Internet and having the ability to correspond by email is essential. To work in sales, you need a vehicle for visiting clients and prospects. To create clothing, you need a sewing machine. What you own can be a key to your ability to pursue the occupation that most interests you.

Finances are an obvious asset. Being aware of what you have and what you need on a weekly, monthly, and yearly basis is invaluable as a planning tool. There is nothing that will pull you out of balance and stop dynamic growth faster than not being able to meet financial obligations. So become fiscally aware, if you are not already, and stay aware.

Financial resources are material, and important. For instance, to become an entrepreneur you may need sufficient capital resources to get started. Or, if you leave full-time employment to work on a contract basis, it's a good idea to be sure you have money to tide you over during the transition.

Your personal financial assets include the money you have in bank accounts, term deposits, and so on. They also include other financial resources such as the equity you have in your dwelling and jointly owned property.

For a complete financial picture, you also have to assess your short-term and long-term debts, such as utility bills, credit card balances, mortgage and car loan payments, and other debts that extend over more than one year.

Do you have educational and training activities?

When you look at your educational and training assets, typically you will review your formal educational experiences, both past and present. And you would not be wrong in that. Your formal training is a huge part of your educational assets and one of your most important strengths, whether your goal is career-oriented or entrepreneurial.

And yet, we learn best that which we teach. It is important that you do not overlook the value of your experiences both as student and teacher. Your formal education will be the easiest to review but does not paint a complete picture of your educational and training assets.

You say you are not a teacher? Well, perhaps not professionally. But virtually everyone teaches something at some point Do you have children? Nieces? Nephews? Do your best friends have kids? If you've interacted with children in any meaningful way, you've taught them something. Do you fish? Hunt? Skate? Play basketball? Tennis? Golf? Then you have most certainly shared techniques and tips with your teammates or companions.

Have you ever had to train a new person on the job? Have you ever given a presentation to your co-workers? Done any public speaking? Each of these activities and hundreds of others that are unique to your experience involve you sharing your knowledge with others. And that's teaching. This is the kind of teaching everyone does, without even thinking about it. Your experiences as a teacher are the most overlooked of your personal assets.

Being dynamic and taking action is really all about getting and staying balanced. It can be amazingly easy to obsess on a project for work or to help your child, or to support your spouse. Be a dynamic you across all aspects of your life. Remember to periodically revisit this chapter as you evolve and whenever significant changes occur in your life. It's a quick and (when answered honestly) accurate reflection of how balanced the dynamic you is at any given time.

CHAPTER 8

Fear—It IS Personal... Don't Mistake It for Anything Else

"Our deepest fear is not that we are inadequate. Our deepest fear is that we are powerful beyond measure. It is our light, not our darkness that frightens us. We ask ourselves, who am I to be brilliant, gorgeous, talented, and fabulous? Actually, who are you not to be? You are a child of God. You playing small doesn't serve the world. There's nothing enlightened about shrinking so that other people won't feel insecure around you. We were born to make manifest the glory of God that is within us. It's not just in some of us, it's in everyone. And as we let our own light shine, we unconsciously give other people permission to do the same. As we are liberated from our own fears, our presence automatically liberates others."

—Nelson Mandela, Inaugural Speech, 1994

I've always thought of fear as the Quasimodo of emotions—misconstrued and shunned. Just where did this idea that fear is bad come from? Who made it a rule that it is wrong to show fear? Why are we embarrassed to admit to having fears?

Fear is a good emotion. It is an important part of all of us. It is a natural response, and a necessary one; especially when the fear reaction is in response to a physically perilous situation. Fear is positive when it causes you to run from danger. Fear is productive and positive when it causes you to slow down and check out an event before you rush in.

Remember that fear is not always related to danger. Most of the fears we all face have nothing to do with jeopardy, which is one reason that fear is so powerful an emotion and so vitally important for you to control.

Fear is counterproductive and negative when it causes you to walk away from what is good and healthy for you. In the final analysis, the emotion may be fear, but the issue is you. The issue is your sense of self-worth and what you choose to do with the fears that control your emotions.

Every decision you make, every action you take will be influenced by your fears in some way. Fortunately, most of our fears are minor enough to be thought of as concerns, doubts, worries, or disquiet rather than full-blown fear.

FOCUS: FIND AND CONFRONT YOUR FEAR

I have a story to share. It's about fear. It's also about belief, or rather, the lack of belief—but I think it's mostly about fear. Not long ago, I attended a three-day business-building event, a Business Breakthrough Boot camp, to be specific. One of the activities that I thought was included just for fun was the opportunity to break a board with your hand. Not my cup of tea. I planned to watch and enjoy the show. Come to find out, it was a significant event and the play on the word breakthrough in the event's title was intentional.

I was expected to break a board with my bare hand.

Understand, I have no martial arts training. I'm one of those women who make a fist with my thumb on the outside. This was never in my most extreme and wild dreams an activity I expected or wanted to do.

I am, however, open minded and a willing participant. I told the Master, Chris Natzke, that I did not believe I could do it. His response, with a great big smile flashed at me: "No pressure, but I've never had anyone fail to break their board."

The smile I flashed back at him was tiny and a bit shaky. This was relatively early in the day the first day and the board break was scheduled for that evening. My trepidation increased when the boards were brought out and we were instructed to get in touch with and personalize our boards. Exactly, I wondered, how did one commune with a board? Ever a willing participant, I wrote meaningful statements and doodled pictures on my board throughout the day.

It was time. We started with a group training in how to move our bodies and shout. Then the first victim...er participant went up on stage to do her board break. Wow. She did it. And then it was time for the rest of us. We split into groups and did several practice runs.

Well, cutting to the chase, it took me five fails, but in the end I did it. And the entire room shared in the emotional breakthrough that I experienced. I pushed through my fears (which were significant enough that I nearly hyperventilated at one point). I pushed through that board so effectively that I hit the Master in the chest and nearly knocked us both down. That's me in the picture.

Failing to confront fears effectively can place a huge obstacle to growth and prevent resolution of unfinished business. What makes business unfinished? Not dealing with the issue, whatever it might be.

Issues left unresolved turn into unfinished business. Pure and simple. Unfinished business can be issues that have hung on for years, issues so old you think you've forgotten them. Or it can be issues that just cropped up within the last hour.

Unfinished business can be related to anything—health problems, legal issues, financial concerns, relationship challenges, career worry, organizational disquiet, business stress or even fear of not breaking a board in front a hundred or so people whose respect you want.

Any unresolved issue in your life, any mess you've failed to clean up breeds fear and can overwhelm you with little or no notice—usually at the most inconvenient times.

Fear. Doubt. Loss of confidence. Lack of courage. A life out of control. The result is a huge drain on your energy.

Most of the time, our fears are controllable and in fact provide a good emotional check and balance on our activities. But the sheer volume of unfinished business that can pile up on top of the stress of daily life creates an excess of the worst kind of baggage, a dead weight draped across your back that, unchecked, bends you to its will instead of your own.

There are several ways to address your unresolved business. You could do one of my personal favorites—pretend it's not happening. It's fun for a while to live in a fantasy world, denying that your problems exist or that they are serious enough to require your attention. But it doesn't work. Trust me on this. Denial results in the worst kind of consequences and none that you would have chosen had you acted in time to have a choice.

"Everything You Want Is on the Other Side of Fear."

—George Addair

You could just go on with your life. Do just enough with the problem to make it seem to disappear and to head off consequences. The problem is that putting your unresolved business into an alternate dimension doesn't resolve the issue. The essential problem remains unresolved and will wait patiently for you to deal with it.

This happens a lot when relationships end and when people we care about die. Grief is unresolved business of the most intense kind, and sticking your head in the sand does not make it go away. This only hides it from your view and keeps you stuck in the sand.

The obvious—and the healthiest—solution is to confront your unfinished business before it gets out of hand. Makes sense, doesn't it? If your problem is that you need and deserve a raise, then asking your boss for the raise is better than moping and complaining to everyone except the boss about how unfairly you are treated.

If you don't confront the issue, then you have no idea whether your boss would agree to the raise or not. It may very well be that you are valued as highly as you think you should be. It may also be that you are not valued as highly as you should be. In either case, it's infinitely more preferable to know the truth so that you can make a decision about your future based on fact rather than conjecture and imagination.

So why don't we do this routinely? Believe me, confronting and clearing issues before they grab hold of our lives is infinitely easier. The answer is most likely related to that nearly universally disliked and misunderstood word—confrontation.

Confrontation is uncomfortable, right? It's messy. It's loud. It's violent. Right?

Not necessarily. It's true that confrontation can be all of those things and worse—take a look at how many people are dying in the Middle East in the worst kind of confrontation imaginable. But I'm asking you to consider the positive side to confrontation. I'm talking about walking through your fear rather than sidestepping it.

I'm a bit of a risk taker and not generally afraid of much. But I have a secret fear. It is unreasonable and I know it. But that does not make it any less valid. I am afraid of crossing bridges. Do you know how many bridges there are in this world? There was a time when I would drive miles out of my way to avoid the bridges I feared the most. And I lived in a valley between two rivers, where it was truly inconvenient and at times impossible to avoid bridges!

Eventually I came to realize that I was being absurd. Other people crossed those bridges every day, so why shouldn't I? It was at that point that I resolved to master this fear. It didn't happen overnight, but it did happen.

I came to understand that what drove my fear was a belief (mistaken) that there wasn't enough room on the bridge for me and another vehicle. I won't bore you with the details, but eventually I proved to myself that there was enough room. I can now drive across any bridge. I even drove down the side of a volcano on a switchback path, which was much higher and narrower than any bridge I ever crossed. Of course, don't ask me about crossing open-weave metal bridges on foot...I haven't mastered that part of my fear. Yet.

The point is, stepping through fears to confront issues simplifies life. We gain confidence, accelerate progress, and energize activities by de-cluttering life through the simple act of confronting unfinished business before it becomes unfinishable.

How can you identify and overcome your fears and concerns? Clear up your unresolved business, then identify and walk through your greatest fears. Here are a couple of suggestions:

- Schedule some quiet time to think. It's important not to be interrupted.

- Ask yourself this fundamental question: What do I really fear? Keep repeating this question, in different variations if you like, over and over. What do I fear the most? What do I fear that is in the past? What do I fear right now? What do I fear from the future?

This kind of reflective thinking improves your mental clarity, generates calmness, and leads to confidence. It is an effective method of confronting unfinished business head-on, or at the least understanding the best methods for confronting your issues.

The keys to stepping through your fears are clarity and confidence. When you are caught in a quagmire of confusion, fear and emotion rule. Gaining clarity over your thoughts pushes away emotional clutter, clearing your mind for calm, confident decision making.

Don't confuse bravery and confidence. At the heart of bravery is bravado, which is nothing more than false courage ruled by emotion. Confidence is not the absence of fear. Confidence is the strength to move through fear following a calm, clearly thought-out decision to do so.

Fear and unfinished business are two powerful blockers that must be dealt with continuously. Be on guard against and aware of the emotional turmoil these blockers wreak. When life puts you in fearful situations, step up and through your fears. You'll find clarity and hope replacing emotional disorder and despair.

Identify Life-Passion

CHAPTER 9

Passion and Purpose

"If you organize your life around your passion, you can turn your passion into your story and then turn your story into something bigger—something that matters."

—Blake Mycoskie

Thus far in this book we have focused your choices and on how to choose happiness as an attitude toward life. We've discussed fear and the importance of confrontation, stepping through your fears. We've defined the dynamic you and demonstrated the power of belief. We've explored your strengths, your personality, your knowledge, abilities, and experiences. The common thread running through all of our discussions has been the search for your purpose and your passion—specifically your life-passions.

You might recall that my two-part goal for your successful completion of this training is:

- To help you find the dream, the passion, the picture you paint of the YOU you want to be,
- To help you develop a mission, a plan of action that will take you to the author-ity and success you desire.

Are you wondering how resolving unfinished business or conquering fear will help you to find purpose and become an author?

Each person has a unique combination of purpose and passion. The reality is that I can't predict what skills, experiences, and talents you will need to be successful according to your standards. What I can predict is that regardless of what your unique definition of success might be, your chances of actually achieving that success increase exponentially the better you know yourself and believe in your worth and talents.

> **Passion is found in the Dream, and the Dream Creates Purpose and Direction**

- **D** Dream to direct you
- **I** Information to guide you
- **R** Reason to create meaning for you
- **E** Energy to keep you going
- **C** Clarity to focus you
- **T** The right people to support you
- **I** Inner peace to calm you
- **O** Organization to declutter you
- **N** No excuses to stop you

- **D** Direction
- **R** Reason
- **E** Energy
- **A** All of you
- **M** Mission

Bring It Back to Life-Passion

This chapter is all about balance. Before you can clearly define your dream, your passion, it is necessary for you to find a balance within yourself. Before you can create a plan of action, you must find a balance within yourself. You must find an understanding of how all of what we have discussed thus far comes together to enable you to find the purpose in your life-passion and take the next step to profit and to author-ity through purpose-driven passion.

It comes back to pursuing that one thing that you keep coming back to. That one thing that gives you joy no matter what. Your life, when filled with passion, will paint a picture that is:

- Focused,
- Resilient,
- Enthusiastic,
- Energized.

Do you have difficulty staying focused and on track? One reason may be that you have no clear plan to follow. Another may be that you feel no passion for what you are doing. Either situation is resolved when you are living a life that centers on your life-passion.

When you invest the majority of your time, every week, every day, doing what you do best and like most, then enthusiasm and energy overflow in your life. You do not fear challenges, or change, or conflict—your attitude and the power of your beliefs keep you resilient and in control.

Do you truly want to control your life? Do you honestly desire freedom in your life? Then you first have to achieve the autonomy only personal growth can provide. You have the freedom and ability to achieve. You have the tools to achieve. Will you join the minority and use your strengths to achieve your goals?

People do not lack the desire to change. They lack a strategy or plan to initiate and sustain change.

Will you become one who creates personal freedom and makes dreams happen?

FOCUS: EXPLORE BALANCE THROUGH LIFE-PASSION

You have the necessary personality strengths. You have the knowledge, skills, and experience. You have the passion. You have the belief. The pages you've read thus far are proof.

What you lack is a plan to make your life-passion pay and be profitable. It is not enough to know what you want to do; you must have a blueprint that shows you how to build your success, and your blueprint must involve your life-passion.

When there is no master plan, you will show up each day unprepared for what life throws at you. The most important part of your master plan is a firm understanding of your purpose, your life- passions, your dreams, your mission.

Each person defines success differently. Before moving on to the next chapter, write down a few words describing how you have learned or benefited from the book thus far.

What roadblocks might you throw up to sabotage success? What does it mean to be perfectly designed for the life and success you currently enjoy? Why are your beliefs so important to goal achievement and author-ity? What have you discovered about your knowledge, abilities, and skills? What have you learned about your personality, your values, and the balances in your life?

CHAPTER 10

Recognize Life-Passion

> *"You can't connect the dots looking forward; you can only connect them looking backward. So you have to trust that the dots will somehow connect in your future. You have to trust in something—your gut, destiny, life, karma, whatever. This approach has never let me down, and it has made all the difference in my life."*
>
> —Steve Jobs

What is your life-passion? Where do you look for it? Those are the questions of the day. Perhaps you know what your life-passion is but are so tied up in the day-to-day drudgery of life that you have lost touch with joy and enthusiasm. On the other hand, maybe you have no idea what your life-passion might be. No matter what your personal situation is, the reality is that you would not be reading this book if you were in fact living your life-passions to the fullest

FOCUS: SEARCH YOUR PASSION

How can you recognize your life-passion? Here are a few indicators to look for that can lead you to a better understanding of your life-passions, hidden or known.

Look at what you do and ask yourself why.

Look for the things you love to do, those pastimes that you find most interesting and that provide you with a sense of fulfillment. Your life-passion will almost certainly have a personal significance to you alone; it will empower and energize you. It will seem natural and right to you and, oddly enough, will be obvious to you once you are open to experiencing it.

Look to what inspires you and that you find inspiring. A life-passion will often have a spiritual side and will provide a service or fill a need for others. Your life-passion will always inspire you and therefore lead to inspiration in others.

Spend time reflecting, meditating, praying. Life-passion is often most evident when the mind, body, and spirit work together. It is a projection of the kind of life you want to lead and are meant to lead.

Become acutely aware of what drives and motivates you.

Learn to listen to yourself. Come to understand your desire to be free.

Given the chance and the right conditions, most humans will choose to do good. Most of us like and want to help others, we want to create wonderful things and add our mark to civilization. Yet many of us are blind to what drives us and are out of touch with the passions that motivate and enrich us.

Follow Your Dream

For many of us, meeting needs, achieving dreams, and embracing life-passions is a matter of chance or luck rather than focused action. Life happens to us. We become blasé and content with our fate. We blame chance and providence instead of taking ownership of our own destiny. Does this describe your life?

Are you content with the life you lead? Contentment is not enough. Wake up. It is time to dream again!

What are your dreams? To own a business? Change careers? Write a novel? Finish a degree? Financial freedom? Computer literacy? Be a beach bum? Have a child? Move to your ideal town? Become a respected expert in your field?

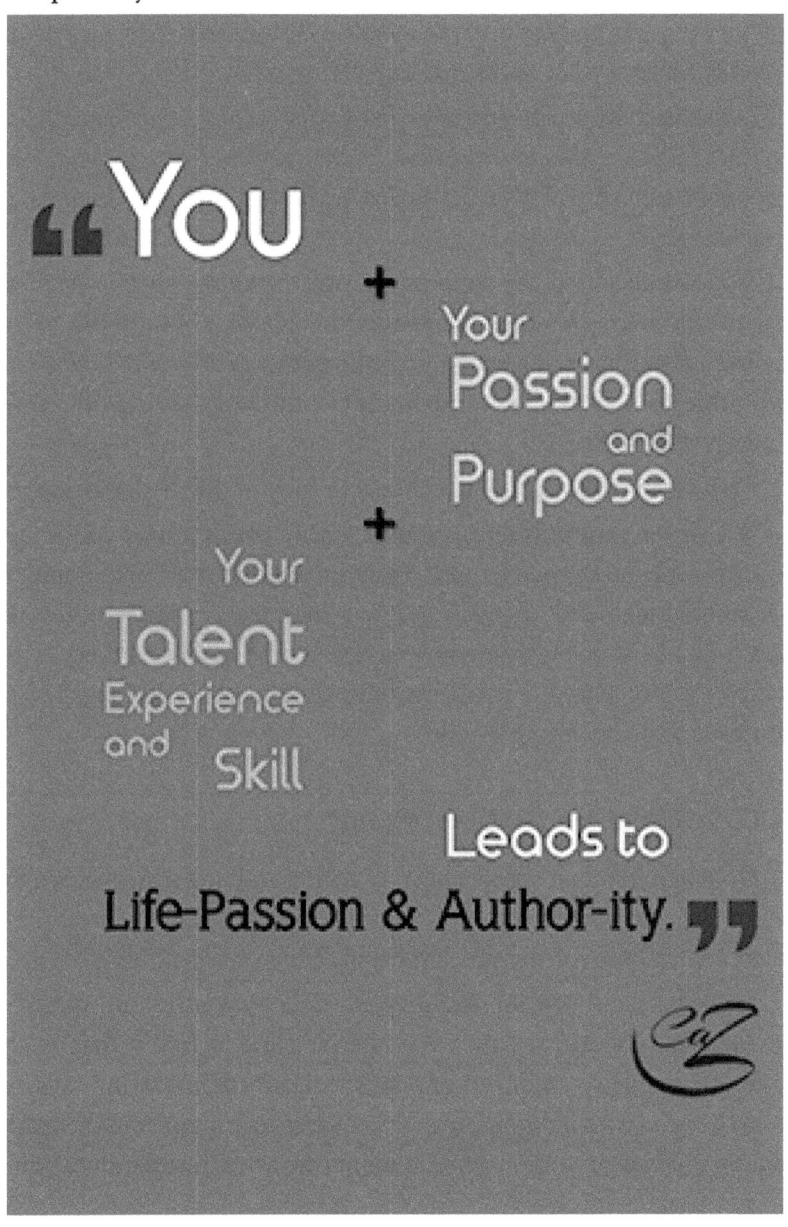

When you allow your dreams to pull you, your passion unleashes a creative force that can overpower any obstacle in your path. To unleash this power your dreams must be well defined.

Every one of us, when we were young, had dreaming as a common trait. The world hadn't gotten to us yet to convince us that we couldn't possibly achieve what our hearts longed for.

Eventually we let our dreams die. People told us that we couldn't do the things we dreamed of doing. People told us that our goals were impossible. Be responsible. Settle down and get a job. Be dependable, people said.

We listened to those supposedly well-meaning people. And we learned the wrong lessons. We learned to take care of business, to live the mundane life, to be content with the reality people told us was safe. We came to believe that contentment is the best, perhaps the only, choice we have.

There is another choice: the choice to fill your life with passion.

Whatever your passion is, wherever your dream might take you, it requires a plan. For many, our lives up until now have been spontaneous, unplanned, and unconscious. You may have stumbled onto the ideal job, but your life's outcome has been predictably random. Foreseeable results require a structure, whether chosen or accidental. First you have to be open to possibility.

FOCUS: SEARCH OUT YOUR DREAMS

Do you remember when you were a child and no dream seemed too big? When any future you could conceive was possible? When excitement and passion for the smallest detail of life was routine?

Entrepreneurs are increasingly starting businesses in search of personal fulfillment, and there's no better place to find it than in the things that you love to do, occupations and tasks that you find exciting. Whether you're looking to launch your business online or in the empty building just around the corner, discovering what really moves you is the key to your success.

Throughout your life, you have dreamed of many different possibilities for your future. One extremely valuable tool for getting in touch with your life-passions is to take a serious look at your dreams, both past and present.

Have you dreamed about being famous? Being a hero? Being a politician? Being widely acclaimed for your expertise? Or are your dreams more modest. Have you dreamt of being the best teacher you've ever known? Of being the best mother ever? Think about what you've dreamed of being. What is so attractive about that fantasy? What are your reasons for choosing this dream ambition above all others?

Take a few moments to think about your dreams of the past. Go ahead. Close your eyes and remember. I'll wait.

Examining your past dreams in this way is a practical method of getting in touch with your current dreams, your passions, your motivations. The activities that you feel passionate about are different than those chosen by other persons. The more detailed and specific you can make your knowledge about your dream and motivation, the stronger your understanding of your life-passions will be.

Dreams contain many clues about what interests you, what motivates and excites you, and what you consider meaningful work.

Dreams allow you to visualize future realities. They enrich your life by providing realistic hope. A hope that results in energy, focus, passion, and direction. When you gain the ability to clearly see your future based in the reality of your dreams, in a reality filled with hope and eagerly awaited, then my job here is nearly done.

Is your morning wake up call an opportunity to start the day just like every other day? Or is your morning wake up call a chance to make your dream become reality? Or do you hit the snooze button and put your morning wake up call on hold to avoid a day filled with wishing for some magic to release you from the trap of a ho-hum reality? The call you wake to every day is up to you.

Will you become a person for whom dreams become a reality? Or will you remain a person who relegates your dreams to forgotten wishes buried deep in your heart? The answer is to be found in your passion, your purpose, your beliefs, your attitudes, your skills, and your focus.

Chapter 11

Lights, Camera, Action

"A bird doesn't sing because it has an answer, it sings because it has a song"

—Maya Angelou

Have you ever read one of those *Chicken Soup for the Soul* books? You know the ones I mean. *Chicken Soup for the Soul* was the first and an immediate best-seller that has spawned numerous Chicken Soup 'children'.

It's a book concept that I've always wished I'd had first. Simple yet appealing. Telling heartwarming success stories, which is an integral part of every public speaking experience I've ever had—from either side of the podium.

All Passions Have Value

Your future success or failure is a decision away. Decisions impacting your life will be made—either by you or for you. It is preferable to make our own choices in life. Yet, we are not equally qualified to make wise and beneficial choices. While the control of our life decisions is always in our hands, all too often we let fear overwhelm our passion. We let emotions cloud our choices and destroy our enthusiasm.

Unless you are a Vulcan of Star Trek fame, like Mr. Spock, none of us makes decisions without emotional involvement.

The power of clarity in making decisions cannot be denied. Clarity provides direction, clears confusion, organizes thought, and opens the mind to new possibilities.

Identify Your Life-Passion

The process we follow in making decisions has been heavily researched and reported. A cursory online search yields five million individual results. Clearly, this is not a topic that we can dip too deeply into in a brief chapter. Even so, let's discuss the basic process.

The first step in making any decision is to recognize the need for a decision. What is the issue? Is there something wrong that needs fixing? Is there conflict to be resolved?

Next, it is vitally important to get the facts. What are the relevant facts of the issue? What individuals or groups have a stake in the outcome? What is at stake for each? Are there important stakeholders in addition to those directly involved? What are the options for taking action? Have all the relevant persons and groups been identified and consulted?

After gathering as much information as you can, you then evaluate your options and possible actions. Which option will produce the most good and do the least harm? Which option respects the rights and dignity of all stakeholders? Even if not everyone gets all they want, will everyone still be treated fairly? Which options would promote the common good?

"Clarity and Decision Turn Passion into Vision and Success"

—Candy Zulkosky

Only now, after identifying the issue, learning as much about it as possible, and considering all possible outcomes, are you ready to make a decision. Yet still there are two additional factors to be considered before the decision is made.

Given all that you know, is your choice the right thing to do?

If you told someone you respect why you chose this option, what would that person say?

Finally, you are ready to make your decision and to take action. But the process does not end with the decision or the action.

Reflection on the decision after action is the final step of the decision-making process. After you act, take time to consider these questions—how did it turn out for all concerned? If you had to do it over again, what might you do differently?

Accountability

Dreams and passion make your life-passion meaningful and profitable. Purpose comes hand-in-hand with direction to create the foundation for maintaining control and making effective decisions.

How do you create direction? .

The dream is the vision. It's what drives you or your organization ahead. It requires clarity to develop and to achieve.

Goals are the plan we set to achieve our dream. Goal setting is useless without a dream.

Support is offering calmness in the midst of confusion. The human mind cannot deal with clutter.

Define Future Success—Your Action Plan

Think about decisions you've made recently. Did you know enough? Did you think about the consequences? Did you postpone the decision until you could sort out the options and make the right choice?

When you know the facts, limit your fear and emotion, gain clarity of thought, and consider the opinions of respected advisors, you are in control of your life and you control the direction of your future.

Direction creates a foundation for maintaining control and making effective decisions. A future with no direction is chance driven by circumstance. A future designed by direction is exciting and welcome. It is up to you to design your future. Let your dream guide you and provide energy to keep you going. Direction is the dream. And passion keeps the dream alive.

Your first step in the journey toward your dream of success is to decide. Decide that from now on you will step through fear. You will discover the passion around you and inside you. You will discover the passion around which to build your business.

Success in anything you choose to pursue requires direction, desire, decision, and deeds. Take your first steps, even if you've tried many times before and failed or even if you've never tried before. Resolve that you will gain the knowledge you need to follow your passion to success.

Chapter 12

Prepare for Change

"If you don't like something, change it. If you can't change it, change your attitude. Don't complain."

—Maya Angelou

When I chose the subtitle for this book, *Profit from Writing about Your Life-Passion*, it, in part, appealed to me because of the word play around the word profit.

Let's talk about the definition of profit. A financial gain is clearly a profit. So too, however, is a personal gain. Recognizing your passions, learning how to move from passion to purpose, and acting upon your dreams are all actions that can be considered profitable. Without discounting the importance of financial profit, remember to focus on the personal profit as well.

The dream, the passion, comes from within you. Your passion is a burning ember deep inside of you, a flaming coal that is easily quenched yet is just as easily coaxed to flame. Only you can define exactly what qualifies as your passion, but the reality is that your passion could be just about anything.

A few of the qualities you might expect to find attached to your passions can be drawn from this list of questions. Take a few moments and give thought to each of these questions. If you'd like to write your responses, feel free to do so.

- What sorts of actions do you love doing?
- What daily or occasional tasks do you find interesting and absorbing? What activities do you find inspiring and think might inspire others?
- What comes naturally to you, seems easy, and makes sense to you? In particular, what do you do easily that is considered to be difficult for some or most people?
- What do you do that is personally significant, tasks or activities for which you have a unique perspective?
- What actions empower and energize you?
- What do you do that capitalizes on your strengths, your assets, attributes, and abilities?
- What do you do that provides a sense of personal fulfillment?
- What do you do that motivates you to endless enthusiasm for associated projects?

By no means are these questions an inclusive list. The qualities of a life-passion are as personally defined as are the passions themselves. Everyone has passions; some are better defined than others. Some people are more closely in touch with their passions.

Take Action and Live your Passion

Where are your passions to be found? Look inside of yourself. Look at your daily actions and interactions with others. You touch your passions every day whether or not you realize it. Excitement and enthusiasm for tasks and actions and a sense of fulfillment are dead giveaways that you are engaged in activities for which you feel passion. Your passions are close to the things you love to do. Tied to the attitudes by which you address life. Disguised as regret for not following dreamed-of paths in life. Passions are hidden in the unexpressed vision of who you want to be, wish to be, can be.

It's Not Necessary to Reinvent the Wheel

Learning to see and embrace your passions is only the beginning. These lessons are about passion and success. Up to this point, we've talked around success without defining or expanding on how to draw success out of passion. Just as your passion is a personal discovery, so, too, is your definition of success personal.

For some, success means fantastic wealth and power. For others, it means having the right someone to share your life with. For others, success is having the ability to help others. And for many of us, success is some combination of all of the above. Success is relative, broad, and unique to each person.

For the purposes of this lesson, we'll limit our understanding of success to mean business and financial success, of the sort that leads to personal lifestyle freedom.

To find success from passion it is not necessary to struggle to create a shining new idea or discover the next trend that will light up the consuming public. It takes way too much energy to invent the wheel and just as much to reinvent it. Start instead by listening to your own intuition. Get in touch with your inspiration. Combine your passion with some basic understanding of human nature, mix with a twist of shifted thinking, and you'll consistently come up with winning passion ideas.

One major key to turning your life-passion into author-ity is gaining an understanding of what motivates people to buy, why people pay, and what they pay for. Everyone buys out of a sense of want, because there is a need that the purchase will fill. The *what's in it for me* factor is at the base of every purchase.

We all make emotional decisions. As we've discussed in previous lessons, it is not possible to completely separate emotion from decision making. In this situation, your reason for considering the emotions related to decision making is different. When considering your ideal business or how you will find success from your passion, you will consider the emotional reasons people buy and how your business idea can fulfill one or many of those reasons. It's all about the benefits if you are the person doing the selling.

FOCUS: ANY PASSION CAN BE TURNED TO PROFIT

Books hold a powerful attraction for me. There have been times in my life when I simply did not dare go into a bookstore because I knew there was no guarantee that I could leave the store empty-handed That's not to say that I always buy books when I go into a bookstore, but I always am tempted. And books are a temptation that I find nearly impossible to resist.

Why? Because I am completely committed (label that addicted) to knowledge. My personal benefit in purchasing books comes from the pleasure I find in reading and discovering the knowledge hidden inside the covers and from self-improvement, gaining the knowledge that helps me to grow. These are powerful benefits, powerful motivators for me to purchase.

Think about some of the items that you buy—every time, even if it means spending the last of your food money for the month and it's only the 10th. What are some of the emotional reasons you buy? What are some of the emotional reasons people you know buy? (Don't be afraid to ask friends this question. It's research for your success.)

Affection? Comfort? Ego Satisfaction? Knowledge? Money? Pleasure? Spiritual? Success? Belonging? Friendship? Self-Worth? Companionship? Happiness? Convenience? Entertainment?

Go ahead and add to this list. If you can think of an emotion, chances are that someone will find it a benefit.

Even negative emotions can cause people to purchase, although generally for the reverse reason. The benefit to purchasing can be to avoid an unwanted result. For instance, how many people do you think really like the taste of 1 percent milk? Especially if they were raised on whole milk? Yet millions buy 1 percent because they want to avoid what they perceive to be a negative action—weight gain or poor health.

"You + Your Talent, Experience, and Skill + Your Enthusiasm ... Leads to Life-Passion and Author-ity."

—Candy Zulkosky

This mantra, this formula, can help you to remember what it takes to turn passion into success. It starts with you and involves you every step of the way.

Discovering your life-passion is intricately connected to the personal development of you.

You. Your talents. Your experiences. Your skills. Your enthusiasm. Understanding each of these parts of you will lead you to your passions. Understanding this same process in other people and how your passion can benefit others will lead to the success you envision.

Steven Covey in a 1997 study found that 42 percent of people feel life is a treadmill and they can't get off. Morgan & Banks in 1999 found that 66 percent of the population say they can't wait to quit their jobs.

But what if you want to keep your hobbies separate from your career? Somehow your passion will impact your career. You can keep them separate, but it will somehow cross.

Can your passion actually meet your financial needs? Your dreams? Well, you won't know until you define your passion and explore the possibilities.

Embrace your Author-ity! Become a Published Author

CHAPTER 13

Write a Book in Two Weeks

"You can't just sit there and wait for people to give you that golden dream, you've got to get out there and make it happen for yourself."

—Diana Ross

There are three major steps in publishing a book: Deciding to publish, writing the book, and then publishing and marketing the book. You've made the decision. Now you face the biggest challenge—writing the book itself.

Is it necessary to spend six months to a year of your life writing a book? No. Oh, you certainly can choose to do it that way. And if you are not comfortable as a writer, you likely will take even longer. But it need not be that way.

There are many techniques, practices, and habits that can be used to write your book on your own schedule.

This chapter describes a process that, if you choose to follow it, will allow you to write a book (at least the first draft) in only 40 hours, working on it part-time as you choose. When you understand this system, you can finish writing a book in 90 days working on it in your free time.

Do it in your free time? 90 Days? 40 Hours? What is being promoted here, some sort of get-rich-quick book-writing scheme?

No. We discussed the fact that following the practices outlined in this book requires effort, commitment, and focus. This process for writing, while honed to an edge that allows you to maximize the results of your effort, requires that initial effort.

The Writing Part

Understand that writing a book means you have to organize your thoughts, set aside time, and actually sit down and write (or dictate) content. There are vanity press scammers who will tell you that you can write a book without quality. They will tell you that you don't need to know anything about your topic. They will tell you that it does not matter what the topic is or how much you know about the topic. They will tell you how to write it and how to publish it. They'll even tell you how to put that book on a best seller list. All for a fee, of course. And in the end, far too many of these scammers will not even deliver a book that meets industry quality standards, if they deliver a book at all.

These are practices you will NOT see endorsed or in any way described in this book or by this author. It is easy to be seduced by the hype, by the promises of momentous sales numbers, six-figure speaker fees, and all of the other get-rich collateral that these scammers toss in to entice you. Here is the takeaway: Do not lose sight of the importance of quality and authority in your book.

Remember what your why is. Remember that you are writing this book to share your purpose, your passion. Anyone can be a one-hit wonder, but for the kind of author-ity that comes with following your passion and living your purpose, you want to craft a book that will sell over the long term, perhaps even decades.

Carve out at least 30 minutes a day to focus on the book. If possible, make those 30 minutes part of your most creative or productive time. For me, that is early morning before the world jumps in and provides uncountable distractions. For one of my writing partners, it was always 2 AM to 5 AM—usually my best sleeping hours.

When you write is arbitrary. Creating the habit of writing is a necessity. Make it a regular habit. Be specific about the minimum amount of time you will commit daily or weekly to your book.

CHAPTER 14

How to Write a Book in 40 Hours

"You don't write because you want to say something, you write because you have something to say."

—F. Scott Fitzgerald

A business book, a non-fiction book, is really something we go to when we are looking for answers to a question or many questions that are on our minds. Let's take that idea of the question behind a book and start there. The framework or outline of the book can be easily created using a lot of questions. It's a simplistic way of looking at it, but this formula works: create 300-400 questions on your topic, answer each question in 5-10 minute chunks (250-1,000 words), and your book is done!

Well, at least the first draft is done. Editing and honing your words will come later. For this process, that is an important point to remember. This process creates an outline and an initial draft. Don't dwell on spelling or grammar. Don't spend an entire 30-minute writing segment searching for one word. Get it down on paper. Read the question. Answer the question. Move on to the next question. Perfecting the text and reordering the content will come after you've got an entire book outlined and drafted.

Start with the Subject

Earlier, when you embraced the decision to write this book, you also considered (and identified) the topic or subject of your book. As you continued reading through this book and explored your passion and purpose, the subject should have clarified. If that did not happen yet or if you've rethought it, then take some time now to decide what your book will be about. Don't be concerned if you come up with more than one idea you want to explore. Make a list for future projects. Remember, life-passions are plentiful and writing books about them can be just as fruitful.

List the Topics to a Create Chapter Outline

Identify 15 topics related to your subject. Select ten topics and organize them. These ten topics will be the main chapters of your book.

You could do this using a computer and word processing software like MS Word, but it's also just as easy to pick up a composition notebook and write it out longhand. Any process for creating and organizing the list is a good process when you follow it through to the end.

Include any extra topics that have not been identified as one of the 10 chapters as subsections within the main chapters.

Now drill deeper. Look at each chapter and identify 15-20 subchapters. An ideal goal is to have 10-15 subtopics for each chapter. Eliminate and combine or expand as needed to end up with 10-15 subchapters organized under each chapter.

This is your basic outline. It will change as you revise and edit, but at this point, this is your bible and you should not revise the topics or their order.

What Do You Know?

Next, write out three to five questions for each subtopic. Keep in mind that these are the questions you will answer when you start to write.

You could put this all in an Excel spreadsheet. Or keep it in Word. Or write it out on paper. Or use index cards. Or a mind map. The key here is to move quickly, giving thought only to the topic and questions.

Do not get bogged down in having the perfect tool to organize your work. I am speaking from experience here, since keeping the perfectionist at bay during this part of the process is always a challenge for me. Your creative process will be derailed and could come to a full stop if you worry about how the list looks at this point. Just write it down. Make it pretty and organized later.

If you get stuck for a question, take a look online or question your peers in your subject area. Find out what they want to know about your topic.

Once your questions are ready, answer them. This is where your expertise and knowledge of your subject comes into focus. In most instances, it should be easy to write a 100-250 or even a 500-word answer to a question entirely from your experience.

WHAT DON'T YOU KNOW?

It is likely that there will be questions to which you do not know the answer. Research these questions and find the answer. Learning more about your topic will enhance your position as an authority!

There could also be questions for which you think there is someone else in your field who has a clear answer that you'd like to include. Quoting anyone else's work, written or verbal, will require attribution and in some cases permission. For now simply answer the questions and make a note of any follow-up that needs to be done.

This process, this system, breaks the book content into nibbles that can be managed quickly. There is no empty white page staring at you. There is a clear outline with questions that need answers, and answers you know!

Have a one-hour lunch break? Take 15 minutes and answer one question. Finished with your last appointment of the day but have to wait for the carpool? Answer one question. Waiting in the pickup line to get the kids after school? Answer one question—you have a cell phone, right? You have a tablet, right? You have a pencil and paper, right? Answer one question at a time, whenever you can, until they are all answered.

...And in 40 hours You Have Written a Book!
GET HELP FOR WHAT YOU DON'T WANT TO DO

But what if you don't want to write it? Well, come up with the outline, questions, and bullet list details, then hire a ghostwriter. The next few chapters discuss how and when to consider hiring a writer and this outline will make working with a writer extraordinarily easy.

Alternately, consider sharing the writing with someone else whose expertise and communication skills you trust.

Either way, once the questions are answered you have a book; a quality book based on your passion and fitting your purpose, ready to take to the next step.

Get the Words Right

CHAPTER 15

How to Hire a Writer

"Life-Passion is the core, the heart, the destination."

—Candy Zulkosky

If you intend to write your book yourself, you could skim this chapter. There's good information on the scope of a writing project, but the focus of this chapter is on what you want and need in a writer, be that a copywriter or ghostwriter.

A professional writer creates clean, readable copy that tells your story and explains your competitive difference. The words professional writers provide for you ensure that what you publish gets the results you want.

Writers understand that you know your topic best and that you are the ideal person to communicate your important message. Writers also understand that you are busy, fully engaged in your occupation every day. That's where your focus is and should be. The challenge you face is both finding time to commit to writing and maintaining objectivity. A good writer will:

- See your topic in a new or different light,
- Draw out the key benefits of your book's subject for your audience,
- Communicate your passion and purpose clearly.

Most importantly, a professional writer will deliver words that get results.

FOCUS: IT BEGINS WITH YOU

Working with a writer is a business relationship like any other. And that is how you should approach the process—as an aspect of doing business.

Begin by discovering how the relationship with a writer typically develops. A small investment of your time (and in this book) will show you how to navigate the process of hiring a writer to ensure the result you need. It truly does begin with you.

Know Your Vision Before You Talk to a Writer

You want a writer who can begin the writing process as soon as possible. For that to happen, it is up to you to arm and even overload the writer with information. You want a streamlined process. You want the job completed as quickly as possible, and you want a finished product that has depth as well as quality. To get these results, you control one crucial factor—knowledge of your purpose and process. Collect the information that your writer will need to communicate what you want said—before you bring in the writer. For example:

- What is unique about you and your topic?
- Who is your target audience?
- What is your message?
- What tone do you prefer to use in communications?
- Is that the same tone you want to use for this project?
- What response do you want from the reader?
- Are there visuals or media elements to be considered?
- Have you a completed outline to share?

Keep in mind that you pay for the total time your writer spends on the project, not just the time it takes to write. Being efficient and prepared before you talk to the writer will keep money in your pocket.

Gather your thoughts and resources. Provide detailed information and have it ready to hand over during your initial meeting. This one tip will keep your costs down, smooth the creative process, and save unnecessary copy revisions. Further, with the inclusion of your rich details, your writer is able to give you a robust final product.

Give Your Writer the Goods

What already existing marketing or descriptive materials can you share with your writer that can be used as background information? Your writer needs a well-rounded understanding of the project, of you, and your topic. Equally important, your writer needs to have an understanding of your history and public image. This knowledge can be gained by sharing marketing and advertising materials.

The writer also needs to share in your knowledge and vision for the project. For this, you will need to communicate directly with your writer. Most ghost writers require at least one interview (in person or virtual) with the principle source of the book's content.

I took on a project a few years back to write and publish a weekly newsletter for a small manufacturing company. As part of the prep work, the client decided that I should do interviews with the company principals. It took a week to complete meetings with these busy executives, during which most of the information I gleaned was detail about current plans and pertinent company history.

My last interview was with the Human Resources manager, who doubled as the marketing guru. At the end of our time together, he handed me a packet of information, including the company's annual report, brochures, and current marketing plan. I smiled and thanked him and managed to hide my astonishment. I had asked for this background and been told it was not available.

This simple story illustrates the mistakes made by this client and the cost to the client for those mistakes. By making inefficient use of my time, additional project costs were created, the initial budget was reworked to include my time to gather the data, and, in the end, the money was spent needlessly.

There's one more cost, subtle and not obvious, but with a high monetary value. Hours of prime senior executive time were burned doing those interviews. Handing me that packet at the beginning of the project would have cut five days of information gathering—time the client paid for at a premium, hourly rate—and eliminated the need for interviews.

Make sure you provide pertinent background information to your writer at the beginning of the project. Depending on the type of book project, this could include brochures, sales kits, direct mail collateral, website URLs, annual reports, research results, and business or marketing plans.

Develop a Realistic Schedule

Writing a book requires planning. Treat it as a project, which it is. Set a goal date for publishing and work backward to create a schedule, including your search for a writer. Your writer can help you flesh out the actual task schedule once she's taken on the project, but you should have an overall time-table in mind before talking to your writer. After all, a good writer will also be a busy writer and your project will have to fit into the writer's schedule.

Take the time to find the right writer. Do it early. Avoid hastily hiring a writer or dumping a rush job on your writer. No matter how skilled your writer is, when the job is due now and inadequate preparation time has been allowed, you will not get their best work.

Give the project and your writer enough time to fully develop. You need to be sure that you and your writer connect and that you have a writer who has the skill to bring your job to completion.

I have taken on my share of rush jobs and completely understand that there are circumstances where a rush is unavoidable. Don't make the mistake that one client of mine made.

Dave

> *The project was to write and print his design company's annual report. This is the sort of project that should have, at a minimum, a two-month time line. He came to me two weeks before the Board of Directors meeting. (It goes without saying that he paid a rush rate.) I delivered the job on time. The client made two critical decisions that led to an embarrassing situation at the board meeting—and forced him to have the report reprinted.*
>
> *The first decision was actually no decision. His own procrastination led to not bringing a writer on board earlier. The second decision was to have his in-house people generate all of the financial reports. This took proofreading the financial pages out of the hands of the experts. To their credit, they created the prettiest financial reports I've ever seen. Esthetically they were a masterpiece. Unfortunately, no one looked at the numbers before they drew up the graphs and charts.*

Revisions are a part of the process as is adequate time for professional proofreading. No matter how talented your writer might be, no writer's first draft is ever fully cooked. Writing, like any creative occupation, needs time to let words and ideas simmer. Expect and plan for one or two revisions as your writer refines the angle, discovers your voice, and conveys the key benefits of your project.

How do you know how much time the writer will need? There is no hard rule. Time lines vary depending on the type and scope of your project. Most writers will require at least a few weeks to develop your copy. Whenever possible, include the writer in the discussion early so that you are able to set a realistic schedule.

Work on More Than a Handshake

The work agreement between you and your writer does not have to be a complicated legal contract. You are not buying a house. However, there should be a written agreement in place before your writer begins work. Expect that part of that agreement will include payment in advance of some or all of the services being provided.

Most professional writers will provide you with an agreement they've drawn up. It is likely to be a simple letter that you both sign. It could be as simple as the quote provided as a precursor to starting work together.

Regardless of which of you draws up the agreement, be sure to include:

- The project size,
- Number of revisions,
- Projected timetable, including target dates for drafts and delivery of finished work,
- Format the work will be in (e.g., hard copy, digital computer file),
- Agreed-upon fee and terms for payment,
- Copyright ownership and reprint rights (e.g., is it a work for hire, does the writer retain any of the rights, does the writer have the right to claim editor or ghostwriter status publicly).

If you have sensitive or proprietary information, include a non-disclosure agreement. A professional writer will have no qualms about signing such a document.

It is equally important to be aware of what might not be included. These details should be ironed out before you reach the point where you are ready to sign the agreement letter:

- Are there extra charges for weekend or rush work?
- Are there extra charges for in-person meetings, travel, or research?
- Are there extra charges for ongoing costs (e.g., a web hosting account for a website)?

Discuss payment options. For example:
- Discuss the retainer. Most writers will not begin work until the agreement is signed and the retainer is paid.
- Expect to pay one third to one half of the total project fee when you sign the agreement.
- Discuss when the balance is due.
- Expect retainer work to be paid for in advance.
- For recurring retainer work, discuss the date for auto billing and receipt of payment.
- Expect all work to be paid for prior to you receiving the final version.
- Expect your initial payment will be non-refundable at some point, often once the first draft is accepted.

Skills and Qualities to Look for In a Writer

CHAPTER 16

Words That Compel

"Writing is easy. All you have to do is cross out the wrong words."

Mark Twain

Simply put, find the writer who gets the words right and says it in your voice.

You will at some point review the portfolios, websites, and various other sample materials provided by writers with whom you are interested in working. As you evaluate their written words, keep the points discussed in this section in mind.

Writers are not punched out of the same mold. Yet there are core skills that every professional writer will have. Combining words to elicit a response is one of the most important.

You are meant to focus on your expertise, not worrying about which words are the right words. Your relationship with the writer begins when you convey your message to the writer. The next step is for you to trust that she will find words that compel.

You can expect a professional writer will create copy for you that is:

- Clear,
- Coherent,
- Engaging,
- Easy to read,

- Enjoyable,
- Structured to spur your audience to action.

What Is Voice?

Whether the project calls for tech talk or fun talk or plain talk, a professional will speak in your voice. Your voice is what distinguishes your message. It's how you stand out in the crowd and touch your reader. Voice is about how your words sound on the page. One reason it's called voice is that readers listen mentally as they read. We all 'hear' the words we read, spoken in our heads.

Voice is the part of the writing that elicits an emotion in the reader.

Voice is a reflection of experience in life. It reflects who you are and where you've been and is applicable both to your business identity and your personal identity. Be sure to hire a writer who understands that your voice can change depending on your purpose.

For example, in this book, my voice is friendly and personal. It is also direct and clear since I am telling you how to find the writer who will choose words that fit your purpose. I should sound like an old friend or trusted mentor, and a little like a teacher. If this was a technical writing project, the voice I would use would remain clear and direct and formal. I would speak in a more practiced and polished tone, with academic overtones.

Your message may not be unique, but the way it is delivered—in your words and in your voice—must be. Words and voice elicit the response, and when we're talking about communication, it's all about the response.

Who Feels Passion for Your Project?

You want to work with a writer who is experienced in her craft. A freelance writer who specializes in training manuals or print magazine articles may not have the immediate skills to create content for a dynamic book. He is likely able to learn, but why should you pay for him ramp-up speed?

On the other hand, experience within your industry is not always needed and is often difficult to find in combination with the other facets of a good writer we've been discussing.

Your writer's ability to write well for the medium is more important than experience in your industry.

Most freelance writers are generalists who write as well for edgy new media start-ups as for a giant corporation. Be sure your writer has experience:

- Diving into a topic,
- Learning it inside and out,
- Churning out great prose to entice the target reader.

The adage "you get what you pay for" applies to hiring a writer. Experience in writing is what you pay for. Your writer is worth every dollar and more.

In any project, the graphics, the medium, and the delivery channel are important—but the writing IS the message. Even a video project needs scripting.

Evaluate Before You engage.

Good copy writing does not come cheaply. Writers charge from $80-$200 per hour and up. Expect to pay more for an experienced writer and one with a particular specialty.

But, you say, what about hiring a writer from those online services where they'll write anything for five bucks?

This is again something that bears repeating: you get what you pay for. In many instances, the writers and designers offering services on these sites are from countries with significant differences in currency exchange, which is one reason their services are so inexpensive. I'm always in favor of a bargain, but when it comes to expressing your passion and sharing your purpose, whether in words or images, it is advisable to get the best, most professional help your budget can afford.

There are a few specific steps you can follow to get a sense of a writer's experience. Inevitably, a personal contact will be your deciding factor.

Take a Look at the Writer's Work

Most writers will have a website. The content is a portfolio of sorts. When available, also follow links to published articles, other client work, and portfolio samples. You will be reading with a critical eye to see if you like the writer's style and whether you believe this writer can communicate your message in your voice.

Talk to the Writer

Initially, contact the writer by email or phone. You are evaluating how responsive she is and how comfortable you feel with her communication style. Consider also whether she asks intelligent questions about your project. Evaluate whether she is tuned in to your project needs. Does she have a sense of humor? Is she flexible and easy to work with without being a pushover? And most important, is she available within the time frame of your project?

DISCUSS RATES

Perhaps you won't do this in the initial contact, but surely before you outline the full scope of the project you should decide whether this person is right for your job and, if so, whether you are willing to pay the price to have her on your team.

An additional note here about when to discuss rates and how to broach the subject. It is advisable to have a budget in mind before you begin talking to writers. Share that budget amount. This is information the writer needs in order to give you the best value for your money. Your writer will be able to evaluate the project after your initial call and determine whether the job can be performed within the budget. Keep in mind that in any negotiation, the first person to name a number dominates the financial negotiation from then on.

THERE ARE NO BARGAINS

A cheap copywriter will give you the same kind of results that a cheap auto mechanic will. You want your copy filled with high-octane gas, not running on empty or knocking cylinders because of bad fuel.

CHOOSE PROJECT, NOT HOURLY, RATES

You get more for your money that way. Writers offer project prices with specific parameters; some reserve project pricing for repeat clients. Project pricing is always in your favor, not the writer's.

If your budget is on the lean side, a writer can bring the job in for less when you make it easier for the writer. Cut down the project time (not the schedule—the work). Instead of a blank page, give your writer material that can be edited or finessed.

Beware Writers Promising Finished Copy Tomorrow

There are red flags to be aware of. Writers are people and the same care should be taken here as in any contractual arrangement.

Fast return can be a selling point. It can also be an indication of a writer who is not busy or is not going to give your copy the attention it deserves. Look out for a writer who:

- Does not return your calls or emails,
- Keeps putting off scheduling your project,
- Does not listen acutely to what you have to say about your business and project,

- Does not ask questions to clarify and ensure understanding,
- Does not take extensive notes or record your conversations.

What You Have to Say Is Important

You know your business and your project best. The writer you hire must get that knowledge from you and must take the time to listen to you.

How Is Passion Important?

Experience is relatively easy to determine by reviewing the public materials your writer provides. Passion is more challenging to confirm. Here is a technique that will work every time to tell whether a writer is passionate about writing:

Ask your writer why she became a writer.

Too simple? Not at all. The key is to truly listen to her response. And listen to more than the words. Listen to the passion that fuels her words. Experience is important, but without passion for writing and the process of writing, you run the risk of getting a cold, sterile finished project.

Your writer does not have to be passionate about your subject when she is passionate about her task. When writing is something your writer cares deeply about, it will show. The reader will benefit from having read your message. The voice and tone will be right. The subject matter will be interesting and richly fueled by your writer's pride in her craft.

Balance Quality and Quantity

Writing is not like piecework in a garment factory. Your writing project is likely to include more than one written piece. You are certainly going to be paying by the piece, even when the project is agreed to as a package price rather than an hourly rate. However, it is not in your best interest to try to get as many pieces of writing for that price as possible.

Early in my writing career I had a client who taught me a valuable lesson about quality over quantity.

Alyssa

> My client contracted for twelve personality articles for her business at 300-400 words each. She produced a monthly newsletter for her clients and wanted this custom content to serve as the anchor. We agreed to a project price and I began writing.
>
> Somewhere along the line, the client 'forgot' that the project price was based on twelve articles. She presented me with a list of 26 topics and let me know that she expected an article on each topic.
>
> There was no malice; she was excited to think she could put out a newsletter twice a month with my content to drive it. It was a worthy idea and had 26 articles been part of the original terms, I would have delivered.
>
> It was an honest error on her part; she did not pay close enough attention to the terms. We did resolve this amicably. I wrote the original twelve articles. And she added a postcard direct mailing once a month, which I wrote for her at a rate that fit her budget.

In most business projects, you use the services of a professional writer to enhance your business reputation and strengthen your customer relations. Quality does matter.

Be sure that you give your writer the time to create a quality product. And for those projects where quantity is involved, be sure to keep in mind that the quantity should fit the project time line and scope.

Don't Discount Chemistry

You need to feel comfortable with your writer in order to work effectively together. You have a business relationship. Your writer will be a receptacle for confidential and personal information. For some, maintaining the balance between being friendly and comfortable with a writer, sharing confidential details, and maintaining the necessary formality in a business relationship can be challenging.

Unlike a vendor selling you parts, your writer will be most effective when she is able to get inside your head and inside your business. When you take the time to find a great copywriter whom you truly like and develop a good working relationship, you'll get top-quality work that will help your business thrive. And you'll have a skilled and knowledgeable writer on call for your next communications project.

CHAPTER 17

When Should You Hire a Freelance Writer

"It's your story and no one tells it better. So tell it yourself. And if you can tell it, you can write it."

—Candy Zulkosky

The last word about hiring a writer is this: Do it. It is your story. And it is true that no one tells your story better than you. But that does not guarantee that you are the person who can best write it.

"What?" you say. "Didn't you just say in that quote at the beginning of the chapter that if I can tell my story I can write it?"

Yes. If you can tell it, you can write. But that does not mean you should. At least not entirely without help.

I am a story teller. That's my role as a writer. In my role as a writer, I can also share in the telling of your story to enhance the experience for you and your readers.

YOU SHOULD HIRE A WRITER EVEN IF YOU CAN DO THE WRITING IF IT FEELS LIKE WORK TO YOU.

Next time you sit down with a writing project, pay attention to how you feel. Mentally, are you quickly and effortlessly able to extract the essence of what makes your offer unique and worthwhile? Or are you mired in extraneous details, unable to focus on what should be crystal clear?

Bring in an outsider, a freelance writer, and get a clear focus on your project benefits.

You Should Hire A Writer To Gain A Fresh Point of View

You know your project better than anyone. A writer will look at your project through a different lens than your own, bringing analysis, clarity, and a strong ability to communicate your message to your audience.

You Should Hire A Writer If You Are A Technophobe

Working remotely is a fact of business life in today's world. Electronic information transfer saves you money, time, and resources. A freelance writer will be experienced in using digital files, software, and applications. It's a smart use of your time to use your writer's greatest strengths to your benefit. This includes navigating the world of digital file transfer.

If you find it a challenge to work with someone in a remote location, look for ways to adjust your work style. Local vendors are always an option but to find the right writer, you may find working with freelancers at a distance to be beneficial to both your bottom- line costs and your time line. You will find that it is likely a small adjustment on your part.

As long as you are willing to pay for it, face-to-face is an option, no matter what the distance. But why pay for a part of doing business that is no longer a necessity?

You Should Hire A Writer to Stay within Your Budget

Hire a professional writer to do what she does best. You would not skimp on hiring the best employee to oversee the quality of your production line, would you? Why skimp on getting your message out?

You should Hire A Writer To Enhance Your Authority

Is there a difference between a freelance writer and a copywriter? The answer depends primarily on how the writer positions herself.

Typically, copywriters earn their livelihood writing copy. The words might be awe-inspiring headlines or plain, everyday language suitable for every aspect of your business. All are considered to be copy. Crisp, professional writing lends polish and credibility.

In the end, it is your author-ity and reputation being promoted. A seasoned writer communicates your message with clarity, professionalism, and style.

CHAPTER 18

Get Started on Publishing and Marketing

"To write what is worth publishing, to find honest people to publish it, and get sensible people to read it, are the three great difficulties in being an author."

—Charles Caleb Colton

Publishing and Marketing

On to the third major step: Publishing and Marketing. What? You don't think your book is ready to publish? You think that it needs polish? You think someone should look at the grammar and spelling?

You are right. All of that needs to be done. What you have is a first draft. It will need to be edited. If you have a good eye for grammar, punctuation, and writing style, it may be that you will need only cursory editing of your manuscript. It is critical, however, that before you publish, someone other than yourself edit the book. At the very least, hire a professional proof reader to catch the mistakes you made.

Yes. I said mistakes. You will make mistakes and not catch them. Putting 50,000 to 80,000 words together into intelligible sentences and paragraphs is not going to happen without mistakes. Get it ready by an editor, copy editor to suggest and make revisions to the content and proof reading editor to correct inconsistencies, grammar, spelling, and punctuation.

There are many steps in the publishing process that can be taken while the book is being refined. Let's start with the publishing process, which includes:

- Cover design,
- Proofreading and Editing the content,
- Laying out and formatting the book according to publication requirements (e.g., e-book, soft cover, hardcover),
- Purchasing ISBN number and barcode, getting Library of Congress number, if appropriate,
- Printing,
- Releasing for distribution.

In addition to these publishing steps, there are many marketing steps to be started, some of which make sense to do before the book is published. For example:

- Reviews and testimonials from authors and other experts in your field,
- Write the Foreword or asking a prominent person to write it,
- Promoting the book through social media,
- Partner with blogs, websites, and other online sources that have an email list or database of followers to promote your book,
- Prepare a website for the book and updating the rest of you online presence to promote the book,
- Direct readers of the book to the book website and your personal website to grow your email list,
- Plan a book launch event,

- Develop marketing collateral, if any (e.g., banners, flyers),
- Get customer reviews online (e.g., Amazon).

In the next chapter is a step-by-step guide to publishing your book and more about the marketing. For now, let's take a closer look at some of the publishing steps.

There are a number of deliverables for publishing and for marketing that have to be produced. Here's a list and an estimate of what each might cost. You will have to pay for these services unless you are able to perform them yourself or your second cousin's brother-in-law's wife will do them for free.

One option that can be cost effective and well worth the price is to hire a Professional Virtual Author Assistant (PVAA). This is a Virtual Assistant (VA) who specializes in book publishing. The PVAA may or may not perform all of these services but will manage the process for you and manage the team of providers that will be needed.

- Cover design - $800-$2,500
- Book design - $1250-$ 2,000
- Inside layout - $1,250-$1,500
- Editing - $1,250-$1,500
- Proofreading - $500-$800
- Formatting Text and fitting into layout - $1,250-$1,500
- Marketing collateral - $2,000
- E-book conversion - $400-$800
- Marketing video - $1,500
- Ads and media kits - $800-$1,000
- Social Media setup - $800-$1,000
- Design and host landing page for book - $800-$1,000

Some of these costs are high-end. Some can be combined. In all cases, you can get the work done for less (or for more) than listed here. Regardless of what you pay, most of these deliverables will be needed at some point to publish and market your book.

Prepare a Budget

Even if you perform every writing and publishing task yourself, self-publishing will cost something. Expect to pay for the services you cannot or do not want to perform. That is reality.

Once you have your first draft done, either written or narrated, it's time to have a come-to-Jesus meeting with you, your abilities, your time and time table, and your finances. Consider hiring a PVAA or Book Designer or Publisher to take the story you've drafted and turn it into a manuscript and published book.

Total costs will vary depending on all of the options we've been discussing here. It is possible to get a full package for as little as $5,000 and as equally as possible to pay $40,000. Be selective, but get the professionals on board in as strong a capacity as your budget will allow.

Publishing A Successful Book Takes More Than Words; It's About Design, Too

CHAPTER 19

A Step-by-Step Guide to Publishing

"Sometimes Only Paper will Listen To You."

—Unknown

Less than one third of books sold are ebooks. Even in this digital age it is safe to say that the majority of readers continue to choose printed books. Have you seen the dire predictions about a war between print and digital and the demise of either or both book formats? It is a great debate. Print versus e-books. The discussion and speculation will never die down completely. As long as technology advances and the desire for digital solutions remain strong among readers, debate will continue.

A recent Nielsen survey reports that new paperbacks and hardcovers continue to outsell e-books. Of these formats, paperback was most popular with 42 percent of sales, hardcover next at 25 percent, and e-books were third at 23 percent. The last 10 belonged to other formats. But that means that 67 of sales belongs to print books.

There is an allure to having a print book that simply has not been replaced by digital technology. Is it the desire to hold something tactile? Is it the ability to share by giving a book? Is it the possibility of simply sharing a printed book in ways you cannot share a digital version? Yes to all of these questions. The allure, while elusive, is tangible. For all of these reasons and more, printed books continue to out-sell digital.

So, does that mean that ebooks are losing? No. Contrary to how this is often reported, there is no war between print and digital. There are strengths and reasons for each book format. Having a healthy market for books—in any format—is great. I predict a future with multiple media formats for books, each of which work together to expand the book market and create new readers.

Both print and digital books are here to stay. There is no war. It's simply a matter of technology and changing lifestyles forcing a change to the entrenched publishing industry. The way the books are published has changed forever.

Does that mean that the big, powerful publishing houses are done for? No. Because there remains a strong market for all kinds of books to be published, the publishing houses have embraced a wide variety of delivery media, including print-on-demand, digital book formats, and even audio and video book formats.

No argument then. Books, no matter how they are published, serve their purpose. Which is what you, as an author, want to consider. We've discussed in great detail what your purpose is for writing a book. And that purpose will be personal and unique to you. At least until you are ready to publish.

Publishing your book allows you to share your passion and your purpose with others, with readers. In these last two chapters, we will look first at the steps involved in publishing your book. Then we will get into marketing it, which is how you will share it with someone other than your mother.

A Great Cover Design

Readers pick up a book as much for the cover and the look as they do for the content. This is one of the most important parts of your book. You must have a great cover design. As soon as you are sure of your concept and outline, start the cover design process. Here's the thing; even if you have no content, once you have a cover, you can begin marketing. Even without any content, the cover makes the first impression.

You must invest money in good cover design. Unless you are yourself a graphic designer or you know someone who is and will give you a free cover, make this a priority in your budget. Hire a cover designer.

The written content on the cover will vary, depending on hard or soft cover printing or when producing electronic media such as ebooks and audio books. In general, some or all of the following will appear on a book's cover in addition to the graphics:

- A compelling title and subtitle,
- Author's name (preferably large and immediately visible),
- The author's biography as promotion copy,
- Recommendations or testimonials from fans or colleagues,
- Barcode for retail sellers,
- Imprint from the publisher.

It's important to get the copy for your cover professionally written. People truly do judge a book by its cover.

Book Design

You have to decide on the dimensions of the book you are going to publish. The most common dimension for print-on-demand companies, such as CreateSpace and Lightning Source, is 5 x 8 inches (width x height). Unless there is a specific reason, which might include simply wanting to stand out from the crowd, avoid going too far afield of the standard. This book, in a softbound format, has a 6 x 9 dimension, another commonly used standard.

Soliciting the services of a book designer or a PVAA can be invaluable at this stage. Either will assist you in preparing the layout, editing, proofreading, and formatting the manuscript into the format the publisher requires for printing.

Expect to pay a premium if you have images, equations, and tables. These added features ensure that editing will be complex.

ISBN, Barcode and Library of Congress

ISBN (International Standard Book Number) and associated barcode is critically important when publishing a book. An ISBN is mandatory if you want your book to reach book stores, academic institutions, and libraries. Even if you are not looking for such a reach, the ISBN helps you look professional.

ISBN is not necessary if you are publishing only on Kindle, iBooks, or any other online platform. It is, however, recommended for all books.

Each media version of your book will need a separate ISBN number. Paperback, hardcover, audio, ebook each will require a separate ISBN. You can purchase a single ISBN number if you never intend to publish in any media other than the original printing.

CreateSpace has an option as well to assign ISBN numbers and for an author who is not planning any additions, this is worth considering. Seek professional advice (i.e., PVAA) as to which option will be the most advantageous to your publishing goals.

In general, your barcode will be generated by Amazon with publication. It can also be purchased with the ISBN number. There are also free barcode generators available online. Let CreateSpace handle it unless there is a specific need to customize. The barcode usually is placed on the bottom right corner of the back cover of the book. Your cover designer will know to leave space for it and the publisher will include it upon printing.

Pre-Press: Layout and Format of the Manuscript

How much free time do you have? Do you intend to become a book publishing professional? Do you know how to use professional software tools such as Adobe InDesign, Illustrator, and Photoshop? Are you a proficient or expert user of Microsoft Word, in particular working with Styles and advanced formatting options?

There is a direct correlation between how good your book looks and how professionally the pre-press work is performed. It is not only a matter of looking good, however. Readability and reader perception are also involved here. When your books is printed and when it is delivered digitally in e-book format, there are extremely specific and detailed requirements that must be met in order to ensure a good result.

Many self-published authors create their manuscripts in Word and for an uncomplicated book, that will likely be sufficient—as long as you take the time to review, research, and learn what is expected and required for manuscript submission to CreateSpace and KindleDirect.

Note that I have named two specific publishing options. CreateSpace is Amazon's print on demand publishing arm. KindleDirect is Amazon's ebook publishing arm. One starts with the printed version, then adds the ebook. Each version will have to be formatted for its specific publisher. And while this is doable in Word, expect revisions. Many of them.

Word is simply not a professional manuscript layout program. Both CreateSpace and KindleDirect convert the word or .pdf file that is submitted to them to an HTML (Hypertext Markup Language) format suitable for their online marketplace and printing options. This conversion from a program that is already riddled with potential error traps because it's not designed to perform manuscript layout and formatting, is guaranteed to have issues. Insurmountable issues? Not usually. Frustrating and time consuming, however, for the novice especially.

The alternative is to hire a professional who will use professional tools. This book was originally written using Scrivener, a book writing software. It was then moved into Word to facilitate reviewers who did not have Scrivener. And finally it was laid out and formatted using Adobe InDesign. The graphics were created and manipulated using either Adobe Illustrator or Adobe Photoshop. The layout was optimized for both print and ebook, thus ensuring as seamless a transition as possible.

Like hiring a designer for the cover, this task should be hired out. A PVAA can assist you in this. Your message is important to you and to your readers. Let the professionals help to provide you with a book upon which you will be proud to have your name.

Self Publish AND Get Professional Help

Here is where I must caution the novice entering the publishing arena. For decades, arguably since the first printing press was built, there have been traditional publishers and vanity publishers. And, sad to say, often there was little difference between the two.

Today, most traditional publishers also have a print on demand arm. Most traditional publishers do not have a vanity press arm. A traditional publisher pays the author, often some or all in advance, for specific rights to print and distribute their work. A vanity press requires that the writer pay the publisher to print their work and, in most cases, keeps the printing and reprint rights.

It can be almost impossible to get printing rights back from vanity publishers and, depending on the publisher and the contract, difficult to get the printing rights back from a traditional publisher as well.

Should you choose to go with a vanity publisher, you have my profound sympathy.

Should you choose to go the route of traditional publishing, this author strongly suggests that you educate yourself and sign with a reputable literary agent to protect your best interests in dealing with the publisher. They will not set out to cheat you, but the standard contracts, especially for first time authors, are not in the author's favor.

What has been described in this book is the process of self-publishing. You, or a company you use, act as a publisher. Of the many routes available for self-publishing, there are two advisable avenues to travel at this time.

This is yet again an area where you may find investment in the services of a PVAA to be worthwhile. While printing and distributing your book is not difficult, it is daunting, with many opportunities for a misstep in the process, especially so for a novice.

Printing and Distribution

For the majority of self-published books, a soft cover publication and distribution on Amazon is the initial goal. CreateSpace.com is owned by Amazon. There are a lot of steps and you'll likely mess it up at least once. There are tutorials readily available created both by Amazon/CreateSpace and by the professional publishing community. Assuming you are computer literate, it is straightforward to navigate, if cumbersome as regards the level of detail required.

If you are interested in a wider distribution, such as Barnes and Noble, then Lightning Source or Ingram Spark combined with CreateSpace is recommended for printing. This avenue will deliver both print and digital books and place your book in the Ingram catalog, which is the reference used by all book distributors and sellers for purchasing titles.

Note that your manuscript will have to be converted to the digital format (e.g., .mobi for Kindle) for ebook distribution. This can be easy or difficult, depending on the complexity of your manuscript's formatting. Digital books have slightly different requirements from those being printed on paper.

Consider hiring a professional to convert your manuscript from the version formatted for printing into the version needed for digital distribution. This is NOT a straightforward process. The nuances and skill needed to output an ebook that matches the quality of the printed book are significant.

Hardbound books cost more to print, but if you are pricing your book in the range of $25 to $30, a hardbound book helps you get that premium feel when holding the book. It is not common for a self-published author to go the hardbound route simply because costs are higher for print-on-demand and you may end up with a few hundred unsold copies of the book taking up space in your garage.

"Yes it takes time to write it, but once it's written, you can sell it for the rest of your life."

—Joanna Penn

CHAPTER 20

An Overview of Selling and Marketing Your Book

"Don't finish the writing and then do the marketing. Start the writing and the marketing."

—Julian Hosp

Bottom line, I can't tell you in one chapter how to market your book. I can tell you that if you don't do it, no one else will. Marketing is an infinite topic and if you know nothing about it, your choices as an author are simple: learn and do it yourself or pay for someone else to do it. The cold reality is that without at least a minimal amount of marketing, your book will be bought and read only by your friends, colleagues, and family.

Ouch. That came out much harder than I intended. But it is truth. Do what you can and do it over time. Your book is going to be around for the long term—you are writing a purposeful book about a topic into which you have passionately invested your time and energy.

Keep in mind that marketing has more to do with the strategies than tactics. Tactics come and go but strategies remain.

This chapter provides a basic framework of strategies that can be helpful in pushing your book into the market. No one can guarantee results; in general, the more effort that goes into your marketing, the better, if only because your book will be in front of and will reach more people, which one expects will bring to you the benefits of author-ity and monetary gain.

Should you decide to pay for marketing services, remember that you will still have to do as much as possible for yourself. Nobody can market your topic or your book more effectively than you. You chose the topic. You are passionate about the topic and your purpose. That passion will come through and will be the strongest enticement you can offer people to purchase and read your book.

Be Seen, Be Safe, Be Relevant

When it comes to marketing your book, you are now in the business of selling that book. Yes, in order to gain the benefits that Author-ity promises, the book has to be read by others.

Gary Barnes of *Breakthrough Business Mastery* teaches these three keys for success in any business which can help you to be successful in marketing your book.

Be Seen. Your book needs exposure.

Be Safe. This may not be what you think it is. Being safe means that YOU musts be seen by your audience as safe, you come to them without an agenda. You must be seen as trustworthy.

Be Relevant. Simply put, to have value you must provide value. You have written a purposeful book. You must put your book in front of an audience that sees the value in your book, in your purpose, in your life-passion.

Checklist for Organizing a Book Marketing Campaign

- Define your target audience paying attention to their challenges, their questions, and how your book is relevant to their needs,
- Create an author website,

- Create a landing page for the book,
- Create social media marketing plan,
- Create Interesting Content to share, ensuring that it addresses the pains of your audience and provides answers to their questions an concerns,
- ASK! Ask for reviews, testimonials, referrals, and shares,
- Post your content on your social media networks and be visible,
- Create ads and place your orders for paid advertising.

Referrals Work

Reviews and testimonials are an important part of any marketing campaign. When you get reviews from experts/authorities, it becomes even more powerful. People try to shortcut their way into decisions based on other's actions. (Yes, when it comes to marketing in particular, there is truth in the theory that humans are sheep.) If others have read the book and found it useful, people will buy based on that recommendation, without hesitation.

Ask for testimonials from other authors and experts in your field then showcase them in your book. When the book is released in online stores, ask for ratings and reviews from friends & family. (No fake reviews!) Suggest that they provide at least a four-star or five-star rating in their reviews.

Social Media Marketing

Arguably the best place to promote your book almost for free is in your own networks, both geographical and virtual. Reach out to friends, family and co-workers. Tell them about your book and ask them to buy. And ask them to share the news! Social media is all about the ever-expanding network.

You can push your book in your network via Facebook, Linkedin, Twitter, Google Plus, Instagram, and any other social media network in which you participate. There is the key, by the way. *In which you participate.* You must be genuine and active in the network to get the best result. When it comes to Social Media, the I in your ROI (Return on Investment) is your presence and participation.

Begin by leveraging the communities and existing traffic you already have. Go to the places where people post about problems you can solve or where they talk about your subject. For instance, Facebook groups.

Take advantage of the word of mouth opportunities your existing followers offer. Remember that social media is not all online. Go to local meet up groups with members who are your target audience. Look for industry events. Connect with local groups and organizations through their social media.

Blogging & Email Marketing

If you own a blog, it makes sense to showcase your book (or upcoming book!). If you have an email list, promote your book with that audience, too. You can build an email list by informing people about your upcoming book and promising them free copies when the book is launched.

Reach out to bloggers in your community or with related topics and offer something free in exchange for reviews. Schedule your blog with posts from guest bloggers, especially if you can bring in a guest blogger or two with a wider network than your own, assuming their audience is your audience.

Put yourself out there as a guest blogger. Provide free quality content on blogs with your target audience. Remember to avoid the hard sell—this is about building your audience and your network by getting your expertise known and appreciated. Most of all, it's about providing a benefit to your audience, filling a need and reducing their pain.

Paid Advertising

Depending on your budget, you can opt for paid advertising on social media, others' websites, or offline channels. If your book is on a specific topic, you can advertise on Google AdWords in such a way that your book is shown when people search for specific keywords on Google. Facebook ads are powerful and when targeted reasonably priced.

CHAPTER 21

A Few Thoughts in Closing

"The key to credibility, to author-ity lies in the quality of the book you publish. Hire a really good editor and writer. Get the cover and the layout professionally designed."

—Candy Zulkosky

When I set out to write this book, I did not intend to offer the chapters about working with a writer. My thinking was that the readers would not be interested in hiring services other than cover design and book layout. As I received feedback from my reviewers it became clear that the availability of professional help for self-published authors must be addressed.

Digital printing and Amazon have truly made it possible for anyone reasonably computer savvy to write and self-publish a book. In the long run, this technology is going to proliferate books and readership. I firmly believe this and there is research that shows this already to be true.

However easy access to publishing services should not lead to poor quality books being published in the print and electronic formats. This author and many others in the business are working to share our knowledge and to make professional writing, editing, and book design services as readily available as are the publishing services.

Simply put, just because you CAN self-publish, does not mean you should. This book, if you've read it and apply the knowledge given, will give you the tools and information needed to write and publish a book. It is, however, a matter of quality over quantity. This is a huge part of my message: Be selective in which writing, editing, pre-press, and publishing tools you learn and use yourself and which tasks you turn over to a professional for help.

My message is simple. Find your passion and make it your purpose. Share your message. Tell your story; write a book. And ask for help to present your story in the best light available.

It's My Life-Passion, My Purpose

I wrote this book to help people share their purpose and passion through publication. And that includes taking away as many excuses and roadblocks as possible. Fear or doubt about writing your story is not a reason to not tell your story. Lack of skill or knowledge of editing, book design, or publishing is not a reason to not tell your story.

I am CaZ. I am the story teller. That's my role as a writer. That is also my role when I work as an editor, as well as when I work as a book designer and publisher. I am dedicated to helping you tell your story.

So what are you waiting for? I've given you the tools. Let's get it on paper.

Author, CaZ

Author CaZ is a writer powered by purpose, so writing a book called Purpose to Author-ity is a natural. CaZ, also known as Candy Zulkosky, lives on a beach in North Carolina. As a technical writer, CaZ has written dozens of technical manuals and books focused on explaining complex concepts in plain English for use from classrooms to boardrooms.

The culmination of her technical training career was spending five years traveling the world teaching computer classes onboard cruise ships. This book brings all those years of experience into a fun and concise package that's aimed at helping writers and non-writers alike share their life-passions to become published authors.

CaZ learned book design and publishing from the ground up working in a marketing agency specializing in publishing client communication projects ranging from mailers to ad campaigns to newsletters to video trainings to catalogs and books. As a book designer, CaZ brings experience and skills honed on many different types of projects all with a common goal: Communicate the client's needs clearly, accurately, and with style. CaZ is a certified Professional Virtual Author's Assistant in addition to being a talented writer and editor.

As a managing partner of Manifest Publishing and as the founder of WritingBytes, CaZ brings the full package of her skills to bear for her authors, along with a team of industry experts skilled in all aspects of book creation and publishing.

Other Books by CaZ:

www.amazon.com/author/caz

Purpose Powered People, Co-Author

Forty and Wiser, Contributor

--Authors Jessica Peterson and Yvonne A. Jones

Connect with CaZ via these websites:

www.ManifestPublishing.com

www.WritingBytes.com

Connect via Facebook:

https://facebook.com/mymanifestpublishing

https://facebook.com/writingbytes

https://facebook.com/communicationtoconversion

www.ingramcontent.com/pod-product-compliance
Lightning Source LLC
Chambersburg PA
CBHW071717090426
42738CB00009B/1803